WHAT BASS

FOURTH EDITION

Laurence Canty
Tony Bacon

Andrew Bodnar
Adrian Ashton
Paul Ricketts

Edited by Paul Quinn
Designed by Tony Mitchell

With thanks to: Ken Achard, Andy Brooke-Mellor, John Burge, Trevor Cash,
James Coppock, Paul Day, Ross Donald, Nicky Donnelly, Ben Duncan, Mike
Emery, Wally Evans, Mo Foster, Estelle Furnell, Dave Good, Martin
Gravestock, Rob Green, Ray Haynes, Andy Heaton, Ian Jenkins, John Joyce,
Max Kay, Christine Kieffer, Mark King, Dirk Kommer, Caro Lawrence, Elyssa
Yoon-Jung Lee, Martin Little, Shirley Lorimer, Chris May, Barry Moorhouse,
Gavin Mortimer, Neil Murray, Mike Neill, Clive Norris, Jeff Parker, Davey
Paterson, Martin Petersen, Steve Porthouse, Steve Preston, Nick Rowatt,
Andrew Selby, Brinsley Schwartz, Mark Smith, Trevor Smith, Marc Snelling,
Pete Stevens, Graeme Taylor, Simon Turnbull, John Wakefield,
Paul Westwood, Bob Wiczling, Dave Wild, Steve Wright, Phil York.
And finally, thanks to
Leo Fender, James Jamerson and Jaco Pastorius

FIRST BASS

Welcome to the fourth edition of *What Bass*, a unique guide to the fabulous bass guitar, brought to you by those nice *Making Music* people.

The bass guitar's importance in musical history is often overlooked in favour of its more provocative cousins, from the electric six-string to the bass synth and sequencer. But the electric bass guitar has been, and continues to be, the backbone of the modern 'band', whether rock, pop, reggae, jazz, country – while the related development of sophisticated bass amplification has made today's bass-driven dance music possible.

What Bass is the only book that thoroughly examines all aspects of this remarkably versatile instrument. It's a buyer's guide, with reviews of 20 of the most popular current models, listings of hundreds more, tips on buying new or secondhand, plus overviews of relevant amps and accessories. It's an owner's manual, detailing the instrument's essential mechanics and maintenance. And it's an historical and cultural reference (if we say so ourselves), pointing out the major names and events in the instrument's past and present, whether makers or players.

What it's not is a bass-playing tutorial book, though you will find a section on where to go for hands-on playing help – recommended books, videos, courses – if that's something you particularly require.

The aim of *What Bass* is simply to bring you and your instrument closer together. Aah.

CONTENTS

WHAT BASS is published by Nexus Media Ltd,
Warwick House, Swanley, Kent BR8 8UY.
Pre-press origination by Stirling Graphics, Southend-on-Sea.
Printed and bound in the UK.

THE
WORKS

Just how does a bass guitar work?
Laurence Canty takes you on a guided tour
into every nook and cranny of the
instrument, and offers advice on upgrading
a cheap bass

The most important parts of the bass are the neck and body. The hardware – the bridge, machineheads and so on – can be easily replaced and together represents just a small part of the total cost of the instrument. The pickups can only transmit the qualities or deficiencies of your bass, your strings and your technique, so generally the acoustic sound is a good indication of an instrument's potential (see **BUYING A BASS**).

NECK

The best wood for the neck is maple – it's strong. Graphite is even stronger and more rigid and, unlike wood, isn't affected by the weather. Because its density and structure are consistent, graphite gives an even response all over the neck. However, this accuracy does entail what some players see as a lack of individual character and a tendency to sound clinical.

Running through the neck is a truss rod, a metal rod to counteract the tension of the strings and keep the neck straight. This can be adjusted when necessary, for instance when the weather changes

–The Works–

(explained in **PROBLEM SOLVING**). Access is either behind the nut, in which position it may weaken the head, or at the body end, where access may be difficult if there is a scratchplate.

A neck-through-body design has the advantage of no heel (the part where the neck would be bolted to the body) and better access to high frets. Because this design involves a longer piece of wood, it is more economical to use a laminate, which means strips of wood glued together. This is claimed to be stronger and non-warping, although in practice this doesn't seem to be the case. Where a bolt-on neck is used, a tight fit is important.

FINGERBOARD & FRETS

The fingerboard can be a separate and different piece of wood attached to the neck or merely the neck with frets inserted. The disadvantage of this latter one-piece construction is that it needs relacquering when refretted.

Where the fingerboard is separate it will be made of rosewood, ebony, or something stained to look like rosewood or ebony. Ebony is best (as well as most expensive, and increasingly rare) because it is dense, giving a better tone and sustain, and because it is strong, helping to keep the neck rigid. This is not news: traditionally, double basses, cellos, violas and violins have maple necks and ebony fingerboards. On a fretless bass, an ebony board is even more important (see **WHY A FRETLESS?**).

Currently, manufacturers have an obsession with cramming the maximum number of frets on a neck – 24 is virtually standard, and 26 not unusual. Fender Precisions traditionally had 20, which meant no top E – this deficiency was corrected on MusicMan basses, which have 21, and I feel that this is the ideal. If you need more, then isn't an extra (C) string the real solution?

The problem with additional frets is that they involve shifting the neck further out of the body, making the low positions, where most playing is done, more difficult to reach. Extra frets also mean longer body horns to achieve an overall balance, distorting the appearance of the body, and they affect the position of the right hand for slapping. Since this is usually done over the top frets the hand is shifted slightly nearer the bridge where there is less give in the string.

A rare 38¼in (97.2mm) extended scale bass built by London luthier Dave Wild. It's tuned DGCF, with a detuning bridge to drop the bottom string to C. Good spacing, good tension - and a capo at the second fret produces a 'normal' bass

SCALE LENGTH

The scale length is the distance from nut to bridge, and is standard at 34in (865mm), although shorter 30in (760mm) scales were popular in the past (as in Gibson EBs, Fender Mustangs and Musicmasters), and a few medium scale 32in (813mm) basses are still produced. The problem with short-scale basses is that a shorter string has to be thinner, and to produce the same pitch, a short, thin string has much less tension and therefore lacks the tone and definition of longer strings.

Why not have a longer scale, you ask? Well, it's been tried with Gibson Thunderbirds in the past, and more recently some Overwater basses, in an attempt to improve the sound of an extra low B-string, have used a 36in (91.5mm) scale. The obvious disadvantage is that the frets are all further apart, which makes life that bit more difficult.

Probably the most significant development in design has been the

9

headless bass. Tuning is shifted to the bridge where the gearing arrangement means more accuracy. And, of course, it's more easily reached. The idea is simple and it's the only one that Leo Fender didn't think of – so he *was* fallible. In addition the neck is made lighter so balance is better, while the absence of a head may eliminate resonances which, when present, can create deadspots – positions where notes don't ring clearly or sustain properly.

Body beautiful: figured walnut used for the body of the Status Series II five-string

BODY

Bodies may also use laminated woods – again, this method can cut costs. It looks good, too, but joins in the wood will tend to interfere with good resonance. A painted body will probably conceal several sections glued together, which will also tend to affect the sound. Probably the best result is achieved with a body made from a single piece of wood. There will be no changes in grain direction, and no glue, so the body will be free to resonate. However, top class single-piece bodies are expensive.

Most of the oriental mass-produced basses have bodies made of basswood (appropriate, isn't it?). This is soft and easy to machine but needs protecting with coats of paint and lacquer. Better, and of course more expensive, are alder and ash. They sound bright without being brittle, and have depth. Maple is heavy and sounds hard whereas mahogany has warmth but lacks brightness. Swamp ash is considered to have a good blend of sweetness and sparkle. Again, graphite is an alternative: the arguments made when discussing the neck still apply, and it isn't cheap. A compromise is to attach a graphite neck to a wooden body and get the best of both worlds: an accurate neck and the body adding warmth. Graphite rods are also used by the likes of Status and Fender to strengthen wooden necks.

The shape of a bass body is determined by the shape of the human body. The design should be easy and comfortable to use whether played standing or sitting – which is why the original Fender design has endured and the Steinberger has faded. Designers try to be original, but if you look at a Status or a Wal or a Warwick, that basic shape is still there. The current resurgence of popularity for the MusicMan bass confirms that Fender's design is fundamentally just right. If something weird and wonderful appeals, remember that when you tire of it and want to sell, you're unlikely to find anyone who shares your peculiar aesthetic taste.

ELECTRICS

The basic electrics of a bass are simple. Pickups consist of a coil wrapped around a magnet which will generate a current corresponding to the movement of something magnetic nearby – in this case, a string. This current then passes along some wires to some pots – potentiometers, if you prefer – which are what you see as volume and tone controls. In a passive (non-active) bass, one which doesn't have an on-board battery, the controls can't boost anything. The volume control can only reduce volume and the tone control can only cut treble. When they're on 'full' (10, or of course 11), they're doing nothing and you're sending the biggest signal to the amp. So it's best to leave them like that as much as possible and set the amp to get the sound you want.

The sound produced by a pickup is affected by its position. Close to the bridge gives a hard bright sound but too close and it will lack volume. Nearer the neck the sound is round and mellow but too near and there's no definition. The most common types of pickups correspond to the Fender types: the 'Precision' is split – one half for the E and A strings, the other for the D and G – whereas the 'Jazz' is a single strip or bar and usually occurs in pairs, or teamed with a Precision-type.

The Fender Precision's split pickup style has been widely adopted

ACTIVE

In an active bass, where a battery is required, there is a small pre-amp, allowing the volume and tone controls to cut *and* boost. Although this is obviously an advantage, some active tone controls lack subtlety and can sound artificial. As a general rule, I'd avoid basses with lots of controls and arrays of switches. Another advantage of activation is that the instrument's output is less prone to noise and is not affected by the length of lead used – with a passive bass the longer the lead, the more the signal travelling its length deteriorates.

HARDWARE UPGRADES

The idea of a new bass always has a strong appeal, but if the wallet won't deliver the necessary spending vouchers to realise your dream, all is not lost. Salvation is at hand – why not upgrade your existing instrument? The suggestions which follow cover a range of possibilities which could even create a new bass in easy stages.

Most of the hardware used on top basses is available separately and can be fitted to most instruments – often as a direct replacement involving no carpentry. This approach is cheaper than buying another bass, will probably produce a better result and can be done in stages as and when finances allow. Obviously there's no point in adding expensive

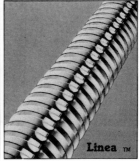

–The Works–

bits to a plank, so only proceed if the wooden parts (neck and body) are good enough to justify the outlay. For example if the neck is uncomfortable and cannot be put right then there's no point in spending money on other less important items.

One initial possibility is to fit Strap Locks (£7.20–£13 a pair) or Jim Dunlop's Lock Twist (£10.95–£16.95), which could easily prevent an accident that would be at best embarrassing – giving new meaning to the expression 'getting down' – and at worst extremely expensive.

Here, in order of cost, are the modifications which will affect the performance of your bass:

NUT

A brass or graphite nut will improve the tone of your bass – especially the open strings and harmonics – and, unlike plastic, won't wear out. Often the original nut is not cut accurately, resulting in uneven string spacing. If the channels are cut too deeply then open strings will rattle; too high and playing is difficult in low positions. Problems also arise if you use a lighter gauge of string than originally intended – it can 'move in the groove'. All these problems are eliminated with a new nut – cost, including fitting about £6 for a graphite one, though you'll need to add about £25 for a fitting and re-set-up.

MACHINEHEADS

If yours rattle, slip or don't tune smoothly then replacement is the answer. The choice seems to be between Schaller and Gotoh (prices start around £40). Both come highly recommended and will solve those problems. The set of Schallers on my fretted bass still function perfectly after almost 20 years – in fact, apart from the neck, they are the only remaining original components.

My favourite accessory of all is the Hipshot Bass XTender (£46–£89, depending on your model of bass). This is a replacement machinehead for your E-string – make sure you get one that matches. It enables you to de-tune it to a preset note – probably D – simply by flicking a lever. If you've adjusted it correctly when tuning up (it helps to read the instructions), it will return to E when the lever is moved to its original position. If it's set to drop down to C then the string may lack tension, and the tuning of the other strings may be affected. If you're feeling adventurous you could use heavier strings tuned down to D G C F, with the hipshot enabling you to drop the D down to a C. Who needs a five-string?

Schaller machineheads (left) and Badass bridge: reliable replacement brands

BRIDGE

Replacing a lightweight bridge with a more substantial unit improves the overall tone and sustain of the bass and produces a tighter and more immediate sound. The degree of improvement is surprising and is comparable with a change of strings. The original replacement bridge was the Badass (from £45) and it's still highly regarded – I've used them for years and we're very happy together. Slots need to be cut in the bridge pieces so you'll need an expert to fit one. The Wilkinson bridge (£59+) is a top loader – quicker string changes – and both string spacing and rake angle can be adjusted and then locked.

Changing a bridge should be a simple do-it-yourself job provided the screw-holes coincide with the originals.

PICKUPS

DiMarzio produced the first widely-available replacement pickups, giving more tone and volume than the standard types but with the added advantage of less noise. Schaller (again) followed with a similar range which had a smoother sound. Next came battery-powered active pickups, which include a pre-amplifier. EMG were first; I've been using them since they appeared in 1983 and we're virtually inseparable. Currently they're £89.95 each or £175 a pair. Bartolini also have a range of active pickups which are highly recommended (their popular MusicMan dual coil replacement is £95) and Seymour Duncan's active Livewire range starts from £115 per pickup.

Any active pickup will give an obvious improvement in tone and

–The Works–

You can transform your bass from passive to active by retro-fitting EMG pickups

virtually no noise in normal circumstances. No more problems on stage with nearby dimmer circuits, and no need to stand clear of valve maps or continue the potentially lethal practice of earthing the strings (and hence you) through the bridge to reduce noise. Bartolini and EMG both offer additional modules to enhance the performance of their active pickups.

If you prefer passive pickups (or if active pickups are beyond your budget) then the Schaller, Kent Armstrong and Seymour Duncan brands are worth considering (around £50 per pickup unit). Later you could add separate active circuity from Bartolini, EMG or Sadowsky (the Sadowsky pre-amp is in belt pack form, and sounds not unlike the sought-after MusicMan circuit).

So a reasonable, inexpensive bass can be gradually transformed and become, in many respects, comparable with a far more expensive instrument. If you do eventually decide on a better bass, then the bits can be taken off and put on the new one – so keep the original parts.

More drastic improvements effectively create a new bass. Replacement bodies and necks are available for Fender-type instruments – both Jeff Berlin and Marcus Miller have used custom necks on standard Fender bodies. You'll probably still need a repairer to assemble the bits and then set-up the bass. One of best ranges of replacement body parts comes from Warmouth (*contact Chandler Guitars, 0181 940 5874*), who ask £130 for an alder body, £175 for desirable swamp ash. Necks start from £175. Remember there will be extra charges for the assembling work involved. This is not a particularly cheap way of acquiring a complete bass so, if this approach appeals to you, it would probably be better to have a neck and/or body custom made. If so, you'll need to know precisely what you want before you start (see **BUYING A BASS**).

B·QUAD 4 ™

IF YOU'RE READY FOR IT.

The B-Quad 4, a visual masterpiece, is the ultimate in handmade craftsmanship. Renowned bassist Brian Bromberg and Peavey Electronics joined forces to create what is being touted as the most revolutionary bass in the industry.

What grabs you first is the exquisite handcrafted design. The body is made from highly figured curly maple for resonance and tone. This is laminated to a center section of rock maple for strength and sustain. The B-Quad 4 has a custom-designed two-octave Modulus® Graphite neck for unmatched strength and stability. The shape of the body makes it lightweight and balanced, and gives you total access to the 24th fret. And believe it or not, when you sit down and play it, you don't need a strap because the bass won't slip off your leg!

A state-of-the-art, 4 in / 2 out, stereo mixer with buffer preamp and individual piezo pickups gives you separate volume and stereo panning for each individual string. The B-Quad 4 is also equipped with two VFL™ active humbucking pickups that can be used independently or in conjunction with the piezo pickups in any combination you desire.

The electronics are extremely quiet and have more output than you've ever heard from a bass before. This makes for unmatched clarity and performance in the recording studio.

The B-Quad 4 comes with four sets of different types of strings. Within minutes you can go from a regular bass to a bass that sounds like a nylon-string guitar. Or change strings again, play through distortion, and LOOK OUT GUITAR PLAYERS!

So if you want a bass with more punch, attack, sustain and versatility than you ever thought possible, and for a price that only Peavey can deliver, visit your local Peavey dealer and play the B-Quad 4. Better yet, play everything else first... then play the B-Quad 4 and get ready to be totally BLOWN AWAY!

TO HEAR THE VERSATILITY OF THE B-QUAD 4, CHECK OUT BRIAN BROMBERG'S LATEST SELF-TITLED CD ON NOVA RECORDS

PEAVEY®

Modulus® Graphite is a registered trademark of Modulus Graphite Incorporated.

PEAVEY ELECTRONICS (U.K.) LTD. HATTON HOUSE HUNTERS ROAD CORBY NORTHANTS NN17 5JE UNITED KINGDOM   TEL: 0536 205520

BUYING A BASS

Make sure you get a good one. Tony Bacon reveals the Five Easy Rules of bass purchase, and helps make your money go further whether you're buying new or secondhand

Perhaps it's the business of having to deal with just those four strings, but bass players do seem to love simplicity. That's why with a few exceptions, the simplest designs of bass guitar, based on Leo Fender's original Precision and Jazz types, have largely stood up to players' changing requirements. So when you go to the music shop or follow up a private ad in search of your new bass guitar, the first thing you should bear in mind is... simplicity. Do you need more than a volume control and a tone control at first? Shouldn't think so. Do you need an active circuit? Probably not, at least to begin with. Keep it simple. You can get complicated later, if you want to.

FEEL

So here we are at the shop. First of all, pick up the bass in question and see how it feels. Don't even play it. Just feel it. Balance it on your knee as you sit with it; adjust it on the strap as you stand up and try it. Get it comfortable. Now feel the neck in your hand, and run your fingers over the strings. Play a note or two. How does it feel? Many experienced players will tell you that they knew a certain bass was a

Pick up the bass and see how it feels...

good one as soon as they picked it up. This isn't bullshit. Once you've played a few different basses you'll realise that there are instruments which do just 'feel right' and drop snugly between the hands. On one of these basses, the particular cross-section of the neck will feel as if made for your fretting hand and, most noticeable of all, you'll be able to play freely and easily, without really giving much thought to the bass itself at all. Which is how it should be.

A good feel is not all there is to a good bass, but it nonetheless constitutes a large percentage. Equally you'll realise very rapidly after you've picked up a duff bass that this is not the one for you. Perhaps they *do* say it's the hottest bass around; perhaps everyone *is* talking about it. But if it doesn't feel right to you, then it isn't right for you. Does it feel ungainly and awkward, do you have to strain to play it? These tell-tale signs will become obvious to you – so take heed. You'll soon find that you'll come to trust these first impressions.

If the overall feel is not right, there's very little to be done. Any amount of fantastic deal-striking by the seller, any amount of pickup-changing and refinishing and general cosmetic fiddling, any amount of spiel from the shopkeeper telling you that this bass is truly wonderful; all this should not deter you from the feel. You're the bass player. You're the person with the dosh (aren't you?). You'll know when the bass is the right bass.

BASS CHECK

And when it feels right, then you should drag yourself away from playing the thing and examine some specific details a little more closely. Some makers or importers are better at setting up their basses than others; some leave it to the shop. Some basses don't get set up at all. The section on **PROBLEM SOLVING** will explain more about this, so you'll be able to tell for yourself.

There is a systematic method you should get into the habit of adopting when you're trying a new bass in a shop, checking out a secondhand bass in someone's home, or just looking over a friend's instrument. With this method you'll know that you've covered all the important aspects of the operation of the bass in question, thoroughly and quickly. This is how the system works...

FIRST: ACOUSTIC

If the bass was plugged into an amp when you checked it for feel just now, turn the volume down to zero. Play the bass acoustically, with no amplification at all, and listen very carefully and (literally) closely to the sound the bass makes. The amplified sound of the bass comes primarily from the pickup, of course, but to produce a clean and clear amplified sound, the bass guitar itself – the wood and plastic and metal that makes the body and neck and hardware of the instrument – needs to vibrate in sympathy with the notes you're playing. So listen for any unusual and uneven buzzes or noises from the instrument itself as you play it acoustically for a few minutes.

Listen to the sound of the bass: pro players often say that a good bass will "speak" to them acoustically. So ignore the puzzled faces of any other people looking on – this acoustic run-through is, you will discover, a crucial test. They'll be doing it themselves next week.

SECOND: FINISH

Take the bass off the strap (or pick it up from your lap) and look over the whole surface – back, front, sides, top, bottom, everywhere. Look closely at the finish for small blemishes or cracks, and examine all joins and seams for closeness and accuracy of fit. On a new bass this will tell you instantly how well the maker's factory has put the bass together and finished it; on a secondhand bass it'll tell you how well the previous owner(s) have looked after it. Any shortcomings here may well be echoed elsewhere, so this is a good early clue to the quality of the bass you hold.

THIRD: ACTION

Look at the action – the height of the strings above the fingerboard. If it's too high you'll find the bass hard to play. So can you adjust the action height at the bridge if necessary? If you don't know how, ask the seller. If they don't know, see the section about setting up in the **PROBLEM SOLVING** chapter.

FOURTH: FRETS

Turn up the volume again on the amp, and put the bass back on the strap (or on your knee). Now play every single fret on the G-string, the same for the D-string, and so on through the strings. As you do this, you should not hear any buzzing coming from individual frets: if you do, it may indicate a misplaced fret, or one that needs a repairer to file it down. Check each fret in this way to ensure a clean-playing instrument.

FIFTH: MOVING PARTS

And lastly, check the moving parts. See that the machineheads work smoothly and accurately and that the controls do what they're supposed to do and don't have any graininess or stickiness to their movement.

—Buying A Bass—

Having done all five checks in the system – acoustic, finish, action, frets, moving parts – you may celebrate by playing the bass for a few more minutes. Not bad, is it? If there are any shortcomings thrown up by the checks, bring them to the attention of whoever is trying to sell the instrument to you, be it shopkeeper or private seller. A shopkeeper should agree to put right anything obviously wrong before you lash out. The Law (*Sale of Goods Act*) states that when you buy something from a shop, it should be of 'satisfactory quality', which means durable, safe and free from defects. You have the right to examine goods properly before you lose the right to reject them. A shopkeeper might offer to put some things right, and a private seller might knock a few quid off if something's not quite up to scratch, assuming that you're persuasive enough to convince them that this is the case.

CONFIDENCE

But whether you're buying in a shop, down a rehearsal room, or at someone's house, it can help if you have someone with you who's a bass player, or at least another musician who's parted with money for an instrument before. Even if they say nothing, but you just know they're there, it can be a real comfort. And definitely worth a drink after. It can also be useful, especially if you're buying secondhand, to have cash with you if possible. It can get you a better price. If you've only once been on the receiving end of the look-at-this-cash trick, you'll know how tempting a fistful of notes can be. And the old shopkeeper's phrase 'discount for cash' still applies. Money talks – so make sure you're heard.

In the shop, don't get flash or start showing off – you're checking out the bass, not the shop assistant's knowledge of Level 42 records. It's a good idea to test on an amp which is the same as (or similar to) your own or one you know, if conditions allow; don't get engrossed in the graphics and compressors of outrageous amps, however tempting. Just get a decent sound and concentrate on the bass.

Consider resale potential. This unknown brand may be an absolute bargain, but what happens when you want to move on to a better bass in the future and therefore need to sell this one? Check out a range of classified ads and see which secondhand brands are popular and what the prices are like – as a rough rule of thumb you might expect a secondhand bass to go for around 70 per cent of its new price.

Buying an unusual instrument? You should take its resale value into account too

Think about this: the secondhand price of a bass often stays at that level, whether third- or tenth-hand, whereas a new bass almost always depreciates in value.

In the end, of course, if you like a bass enough, then go for it whatever the name on the head. You may start a trend – though it's unlikely. Bear in mind that your style might change or the type of music you play might change – and how versatile is the bass you're thinking of buying? Go for simplicity, but try also to think ahead.

And remember that just because a certain bass is more expensive than another that does not necessarily mean it's better. Pricing of new basses can seem to work in a mysterious way; fashion and the desirability of certain brand names can be just as big a factor in the price of a bass as the cost of production and the relative attention to detail. Either way, you won't get any bass these days for much under £100 – and you can pay £1500 or more for a new bass if you want.

See the **BASS MARKET** section at the back for a guide to some currently available new basses; but bear in mind that you'll nearly always get better value for money from a secondhand bass. Remember, too, that a £300 bass might suit your playing and style better than a £900 bass – and that the £900 bass won't necessarily be three times as good as the £300 one.

If you're thinking of spending a lot of money – say over £900 – then you should also consider getting a guitar maker to build you a bass by hand, to your requirements. Perhaps there's a local maker you've heard about and whose work you may have seen and, with luck, tried? On the plus side, a handsome bass will be built to your own spec, and should in theory be an absolutely ideal instrument. It's also very satisfying to watch your own plans change into a real instrument, stage by stage. On the debit side, if and when you want to buy something new, it may prove hard to sell such a personal instrument; and if you don't have a very clear idea of exactly what sort of bass you want when you go to a maker, you may end up with an instrument that even you don't like. So consider the handmade option, but consider it carefully.

Whatever sort of bass you're looking for, it's always a good idea to try as many basses as you can in any circumstances. If a casual acquaintance in another local band has a type of bass you've never tried, find some way of getting a go on it. If the local shop has a new delivery of brand new basses, or has a batch of secondhand stock just in, get in there, chat with the assistants, and get a go on them (the basses, not the assistants – leave them to their speed-metal licks in the back room). If there's a music fair on near you, or a shop is holding an open evening for a particular manufacturer, then get down there and try out the basses. Don't rely solely on rumours and the prejudices of other players – find out for yourself what these basses are like.

Read reviews in the magazines, by all means, but get your hands on these instruments for yourself whenever possible and see what they're like. There's no substitute. Of course that's not to say that the opinions of others are not important. It's worth listening to what bassists have to say – either directly, or in magazine interviews – and it's especially useful to hear the views of experienced players who have been through a lot of basses. But remember that a few bassists appear in endorsement ads without intending to play an instrument exclusively, and that pros' stage and studio basses are occasionally worked on and modified, sometimes to the extent that the bass may not sound much like a stock instrument.

In the past few years there has been some dispute in the trade over so-called 'grey imports' – new instruments which have usually been imported direct to a shop, bypassing the normal UK distributor. The immediate attraction to us is the lower price of these rogue imports; the difficulties arise if you need to get something fixed or sorted out later. While the practice is not actually illegal, official distributors point out that if you don't get an official guarantee card with your new bass, then you will not get the benefit of service facilities from them. You have been warned.

SECONDHAND EXTRAS

When you're buying a secondhand bass – usually through a classified ad, or in the used secion at the local shop – you have to exercise extra vigilance. People have been known to abuse and neglect basses. And then sell them. So in addition to our famous five checks for new basses, all of which obviously still apply to used basses, it's worth bearing in mind a few extra checks for secondhand instruments.

LISTEN FOR CRACKLES
When you play the bass through an amp, fiddle with the controls and listen carefully. Keep your ears open for pickups cutting-out, and ensure you're getting equal volume from each string. Any unwanted noise in this area indicates dodgy wiring or worn-out components inside. If you're faced with a bass with two or more pickups and aren't sure whether all the pickups are working, hold a vibrating tuning fork over each and listen for an amplified note from the speaker.

TAKE A TUNER
A tuner can be a useful object to take along to test a secondhand bass. Make sure the bass is at proper pitch – if the seller is demonstrating it with slackened strings, s/he may be trying to hide something.

Thinking of secondhand? Tread softly, and carry a tuner...

–Buyiŋ A Bass–

SCRUTINISE SCREWS

Screws are good clues to the general condition of a used bass and how well or badly it's been treated. First, are they all there? Check especially for missing screws on the machineheads (they'll soon pull away and affect tuning accuracy), and check that there is a full complement of screws on the scratchplate and pickup surrounds. Second, check the condition of the existing screws. Have they been burred down and made next to useless? This is an irritating guide to a careless owner, rather than a fatal error. But it implies that other, unseen things could be wonky, too.

BEWARE OF MODS

Modifications, usually known as 'mods', might be there to make the bass look nicer – or they might be there to hide something. There is a legendary example often quoted in the *Making Music* office of a bass which went into a 'top' repair workshop to have the neck shaved down. Back it came suitably shaved, and with an extra stripe painted up the back of the neck (not asked for). How pretty, thought the owner – until the truss rod, carelessly exposed by the shaving and 'hidden' by the new stripe, gradually edged its way out of the back of the neck. Be careful, OK?

BE PATIENT

And finally, if you're *at all* unsure, then wait. Of course it's tempting to spend now: you've actually made the visit to the shop and here you are with the bass in your hands. Or you've gone through all the hassle of ringing up someone from an ad and here you are at their place. You're itching to own a bass. But be patient. Are you sure you're absolutely satisfied? There are plenty more basses, but you've only got so much money. Don't let the shopkeeper or advertiser talk you round if you're not entirely sure. Don't be intimidated by the seller. In the case of shops, return to those that are good, and tell useless shops why you won't be coming back.

After all this checking out of feel and quality, you're probably feeling a bit whacked. So have a quick rest... now that you've got yourself a decent bass at a good price (haven't you?), the fun is only just beginning.

THE FAMOUS FIVE!

A N D ONLY £3.95 E A C H

Including post & packing

MAKING MUSIC WITH EFFECTS (2nd edition)

What they do, and what to do with them - a guide to getting peak performance from your pedals and results from your rack.

MAKING MUSIC WITH AMPS & PA

Everything you need to know about getting loud with PA and backline amps: hiring and buying, set-ups and settings.

amps & pa

A MUSICIAN'S MANUAL

MAKING MUSIC WITH

COMPUTERS & SOFTWARE

THE MUSICIANS' GUIDE

WHAT CAN MUSIC SOFTWARE DO?

SEQUENCING EXPLAINED

SCOREWRITING OPTIONS

SOFTWARE ROUNDUP

CHOOSING THE RIGHT COMPUTER

SOFTWARE VOCABULARY A-Z

MAKING MUSIC WITH COMPUTERS & SOFTWARE

For musicians: quite simply the best guide to using computers for music-making, at any level.

microphones

A MUSICIAN'S MANUAL

acoustic guitars

MANUAL

MAKING MUSIC WITH MICROPHONES

Which microphone should you use, and where should you stick it? A definitive guide to choosing and using.

MAKING MUSIC WITH ACOUSTIC GUITARS

How they're made, why they sound the way they do, and picking the right box for your budget. (Co-written by Adrian Legg.)

To buy any of these, complete the coupon and send it with a cheque/PO to: F5, Making Music, 50 Doughty Street, London WC1N 2NG. Cheques payable to Nexus Media Ltd (Overseas orders accepted only by Mastercard/Visa or Sterling cheques drawn on a British bank. Overseas buyers (inc Eire) add £1 each for post and packing.) Allow 21 days for delivery. Access and Visa cardholders can use our Hotline, 0171 404 7770. Feel free to photocopy this form.

Enter your details below and send to: **Famous Five, Making Music, 50 Doughty Street, London WC1N 2NG.**

Please send the following (tick box) ☐ Making Music With Amps & PA ☐ Making Music With Computers & Software
☐ Making Music With Microphones ☐ Making Music With Acoustic Guitars ☐ Making Music With Effects

Price per book £3.95 inc. p&p (Eire and overseas £4.95 per book inc. p&p)

I enclose cheque/PO for £ .... made payable to Nexus Media Ltd or debit my Access/Visa card

No ☐☐☐☐☐☐☐☐☐☐☐☐☐☐☐☐ Expiry date .... Total ....

Signature .... Name ....

Address ....

.... Postcode ....

DATA PROTECTION: AS A SERVICE TO READERS WE OCCASIONALLY MAKE OUR CUSTOMER LISTS AVAILABLE TO COMPANIES WHOSE PRODUCTS AND SERVICES WE FEEL MAY BE OF INTEREST. IF YOU DO NOT WISH TO RECEIVE SUCH MAILINGS PLEASE TICK THE BOX ☐

PROBLEM SOLVING

Your bass probs will come in two main
shapes – the physical set-up of the
instrument, and its electrical workings.
Laurence Canty sorts you out in
both areas

The most basic problem requiring solution is the set-up of the bass, which involves adjusting the bridge and neck so that the action – the gap between the strings and the frets – is just right. If it's too high, then playing becomes difficult; if it's too low, the strings will rattle and buzz on the frets. So here's a step-by-step, easy-to-follow, do-it-yourself, hyphenated-guide to setting-up your bass guitar.

The object of the set-up is to get the action just right

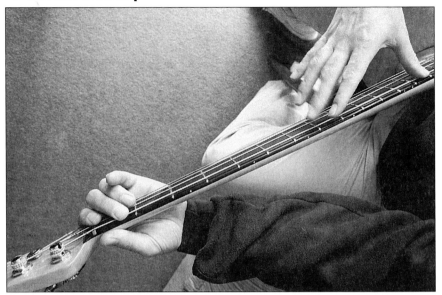

Tapping strings at the 13th fret to check neck adjustment

Truss rod access is usually via a headstock plate, visible beneath the fingers here

THE SET-UP

You can raise and lower the strings by adjusting the bridge saddles, but if the neck is not correctly adjusted you could be wasting your time – even if you improve the set-up, you won't get it perfect. The neck isn't supposed to be absolutely straight but nor should it be warped and approximate to a banana.

To check that it has the correct amount of relief – that is, the amount of deviation from total straightness – tune up and then fret a string at the first fret. Then with your right-hand thumb, fret at the 13th fret. Now tap the string about half-way between those two points. The gap should be only just visible, but big enough to produce a clear tapping sound. If it doesn't, you'll need to make some adjustments.

Adjusting the neck involves changing the tension on the truss rod. Access to this is achieved either by removing a small plate beside the nut – usually held in place by three small screws – or at the opposite end of the neck, often from a slot cut in the body. Usually the truss rod needs tightening to straighten the neck and this is done by turning it clockwise. If the neck is too straight – gap too small or non-existent – then the truss rod needs slackening by turning anti-clockwise. With most basses this requires a hexagonal wrench (aka allen key) which should have been supplied if you bought the bass new (and probably wasn't if you got it secondhand). So if you have the appropriate tool, read on. Otherwise it's time to make a trip to your local hardware shop.

When you're ready to make the adjustment, give it only a quarter turn – and remember how much and which way in case it's wrong. Now retune and check the neck again and, if necessary, repeat the process until the neck passes the test described earlier. When that's complete, the neck should be as well-adjusted as it is possible to be without major surgery. Now it's time to look at...

THE BRIDGE

The first step is to adjust the heights of the bridge saddles. Again this usually involves an allen key, but this time a much smaller version. Before you make another trip to the shops, check ahead to see if you'll be needing another one for the string length adjustment. The basic idea is to lower the strings as much as possible without producing fret noise

Bridge saddles can normally be adjusted individually for height and intonation

when you play. It's a process of trial and error and with each try you'll have to retune and then check every fret.

If the action is still high, the frets need attention and this is a job for an expert. Ask around for advice on reputable and reliable repairers – I prefer to go to an individual rather than a larger concern so I know who's going to do the job.

INTONATION

Intonation involves adjusting the lengths of the strings so that every fretted note is in tune. String length is adjusted by moving the bridge saddles forwards or backwards as necessary. If you don't own a tuner, this would be a good time to buy one, or if that's not possible, try to borrow one.

First, check that the string is in tune. It's best to use fifth fret harmonics for this (plucking a string while touching it lightly at the fifth fret) – they are the same notes as the open strings but two octaves higher. Now check some fretted notes on the tuner, starting with the 12th fret and then some higher notes because bridge adjustment becomes more critical as you go higher. If these notes are sharp, the string is too short and the saddle must be pulled back towards the bridge. If they are flat, it's too long and the saddle must be moved out. Again, trial and error is involved and you must retune each time until you can play in tune in any position and on any string.

Sometimes you might find that if the bridge saddle is being pulled back, the adjustment seems to have no effect. This is because there is a kink in the string where it originally passed over the bridge and it's still vibrating from there. Simply push it down with a thumb to straighten it out, then retune and check again.

ELECTRICAL PROBLEMS

Now having sorted out the mechanics of the bass it's time to plug in and switch on... and do you notice a rather annoying buzzing sound? This could be a wasp in your ear, but closer investigation reveals it's coming from the amp and disappears when the bass is turned down. This is electrical interference, received by the pickups from nearby circuitry such as dimmers or other equipment – your amp being the obvious culprit. If you move away or point your bass in a different direction the problem may reduce; turning the tone control down will help, but it will cut the brightness too.

The complete solution is to replace your pickups (see **THE WORKS**) with higher quality units designed to reject noise. A less satisfactory but much cheaper approach is to 'screen' the bass. This involves conductive paint or tape which is applied to all internal surfaces – the pickup recesses and control cavity – and then connected to earth through the screen of your lead. Although it is a job you can do yourself, it does involve taking pickups out and controls off, so if you're unsure of your skills in that direction, it's better to pay an expert to do it for you.

NO SOUND?

Now for electrical problems which demand urgent and immediate attention – the crucial gig is about to start but your gear won't. The basic advice is *don't panic* – at least not yet – and start by checking the obvious. For example, if you've plugged in and switched on and no sound is produced, the first step is, by a process of elimination, to

–Problem Solving–

identify which piece of equipment is faulty. Disconnect any effects. Still nothing? Try a different lead. Listen to the speaker – is there any hiss? Switch speaker leads. Plug the bass into an amp that *is* working or plug an instrument that *is* working into your amp. By now you should know were the fault is.

If the amp is the culprit the obvious check is the fuses. On the back of the amp you should find a fuse cover which can be unscrewed releasing the fuse. Replace it with the correct value spare – notice that you carry not only spare leads but fuses and screwdrivers. Obviously it's probably not practical to carry a spare amp or bass but take a duplicate of everything else – including strings. Meanwhile back to the amp. With luck it should now be working, but if not, check the internal fuses. This will involve getting inside the amp – after you've disconnected it from the mains – and changing the fuse/s. Unless you're an electronics wizard – in which case you don't need to read this anyway – that's as far as you can go. So if you still haven't solved the problem, *now* you can panic, and borrow or share an amp until you can get yours to a professional repairer.

WIRING

If the problem is the bass, it's usually something simple like a disconnected wire. Provided you've got a soldering iron and solder (that's in addition to all the previously mentioned spares), the repair shouldn't take long. However, that assumes you know how to solder – not difficult and easily practised – and that you're familiar with the wiring of your bass. If you've never peered inside, now's the time to try. Access usually involves removing a few screws. With a passive bass, all you'll find inside are two or three pots (the things connected to the control knobs), some connecting wires, and a jack socket, and as in most cases repair is simply a matter of reconnecting a stray wire, a basic understanding of how your bass is connected up is essential.

The same fault-finding applies to an active bass except that the first thing to check is the battery – naturally you carry a spare. If the fault is in the active circuitry, then it's a pro job and your only hope is that you can switch to a passive mode. If the bass is making disturbing noises, it may be a faulty battery – try tapping the battery on each side, including the bottom, and squeezing it, to see if it's causing the problem.

If the fault is in the speaker cabinet, the repair will either be simple or impossible. If a wire has become disconnected from the terminal of a speaker, it's usually a simple matter to reconnect it.

No sound? Access plates can easily be removed to check whether a wire is loose

However, if the speaker itself has developed a fault or has been damaged, it will need expert attention and you'll have to organise a replacement to help you make it through the night.

LEADS

Leads are probably the most easily damaged item and can easily be checked to see if wires are about to disconnect themselves. Simply open the jack plug and have a quick look inside – you should, of course, have resisted buying leads with those nasty moulded jacks which are totally inaccessible. If the lead itself is noisy, you may be able to isolate the damaged section, remove it, and end up with one which is shorter but reliable. However, when a lead gets noisy it usually means that its days are numbered and the only course is to scrap it before it breaks down completely. But all is not lost. If the jacks are in good nick, a cheap way of getting a new lead is to buy the required length of cable and re-use the jacks – and this is a good time to practise your soldering. But once again, if you're not sure, ask or pay someone competent to do it for you.

PREVENTION...

Where possible, it's a good idea to anticipate problems by carrying spares and the necessary tools. But an even better idea is to find the fault before it causes a crisis at a gig or means expensive wasted time in the rehearsal room or studio. Obviously, if you look after your equipment, it won't get damaged and is less likely to go wrong.

WHY A FRETLESS?

Why do fretless basses sound the way they
do? And are they more difficult to play
than the usual fretted variety? Tell us,
Laurence Canty:
Why a fretless?

The simple answer is "because it sounds different and I like it". But the original reason for the existence of the fretless bass was to enable the bass guitarist to get closer to the sound of the double bass – a warmer tone, notes which 'swell', smooth slides and vibrato to add colour.

The opposite, in a sense, of the original concept of Leo Fender's 'Precision' bass. Ironically the process has now gone full circle and double bass players, with the help of amplification, are being influenced by the sound of the electric fretless bass guitar.

Initially, fretless basses were used with flatwound strings which produced a sound lacking definition and without the ability to cut through. The instantly recognisable contemporary fretless sound is largely the inevitable result of using roundwound strings, a combination originated by the player still most associated with the instrument, Jaco Pastorius. Even on his earliest recording, 'Bright Size Life' with Pat Metheny in December 1975, the qualities of the fretless are apparent, and it's surprising that it took so long for it to reach more commercial areas.

Gradually, the distinctive fretless sound appeared more frequently, but it was Paul Young's "Wherever I Lay My Hat" (1983),

–Why A Fretless?–

featuring Pino Palladino on bass, which finally brought it to the attention of Joe and Jo Public.

Many bassists steer clear of fretlesses, arguing that it's impossible not to sound like Pastorius. Others refuse to slap for similar 'it-all-sounds-the-same' reasons. Although there is a point in these views, it's worth noting that no one refuses to play *fretted* despite the fact that we all sound the same (well, almost). Furthermore, Pastorius sounded like Pastorius on fretted bass too.

If these considerations have not dissuaded you from playing fretless, there are other, more practical considerations which might.

Whereas any decent fretted bass is playable, even if not entirely ideal, a fretless is a much more personal instrument, and I have yet to find an 'off the peg' model that I've felt comfortable with. Manufacturers seem to view a fretless as simply a fretted bass without the frets – a reasonable assumption, you might think, but in fact quite wrong. The fingerboard of a fretless is much more important than that of a fretted bass – it must be hard to withstand wear from the strings, and dense to produce the characteristic sustained sound.

A lacquered maple fingerboard just doesn't work and feels terrible (yes, I know Sting used to play one). What all this adds up to is ebony, but this is expensive and difficult to work (not to mention highly endangered as a species), so is unlikely to come as standard on cheaper basses. The cost (at least £150) of putting an ebony fingerboard onto an existing bass means it's only worth doing to a decent instrument. (Some makers offer a hard synthetic alternative, Ebanol.)

If you find a bass worth converting, then think about the shape of the fingerboard. When my first fretless was built, I didn't have the benefit of this advice and requested that the fingerboard have the same curvature as my fretted... and then spent a couple of years being uncomfortable on it. I discovered my mistake when I played a de-fretted Fender fitted with a rounder fingerboard which instantly felt better. Before ordering my second fretless I played several 'conversions' and had my favourite measured so that my fingerboard would be identical. More recently I've had owners of expensive fretless basses having their fingerboards reshaped to match mine.

It may seem a minor detail, but consider the position markers. Some makers put position dots where the frets would normally be, which is very confusing – and not much help, because not every fret is marked. The other extreme is white lines across the fingerboard instead of frets: this spoils the appearance, doesn't make you look clever, and

Why a fretless? Because it's a jungle out there, of course...

anyway encourages you to rely on eyes rather than ears. I use a compromise: the usual dots in the usual places and lines corresponding to the frets, but only on the side of the neck.

Whatever system of markers you use, they are only a guide, because, unless you are looking directly down, it's very difficult to judge. Even if your finger is in the correct place, roll it slightly one way or the other and the note alters dramatically – plug into a tuner and just see how much the note changes. Often, fretless playing involves fingering higher up the neck, and here accuracy becomes even more critical and almost impossible to judge visually. The only way is to use your ears, and if you're a little out then some tasteful vibrato will disguise the fact. This doesn't mean pulling the string up and down, guitar fashion, but rock 'n' rolling it from side to side along the string – watch a classical string player to get the idea.

So if you learn to play in tune – which means you must be able to hear yourself and the other players – and you develop a vibrant vibrato, fretless playing will make you a better musician and so a better bass player. Your hearing will become more acute and the instrument will encourage you to be more sensitive tonally and create more melodic lines.

The Canty semi-fretless – a fretless with seven frets added at the bottom end

Position markers are personal: the Canty fretless has fret markers on the side only

Finally I'll mention a somewhat risky experiment I tried a few years ago. I had seven frets put on my fretless. The reason was simple. Playing freelance in situations where there was no time to change bass between numbers, I inevitably took my fretted bass and left the fretless at home to gather dust and possibly moss. Having some frets put on the fretless meant that I could play fretted and fretless on the same instrument – seven frets gives enough fretted range to play most songs and still leaves the middle and top of the neck fretless for the higher, melodic playing. Obviously it's a compromise – no low fretless or high fretted – but I now use my semi-fretless more than my fretted, and wonder about the possibilities of applying the idea to a five or six-string bass.

STRINGS

A new set can change your tone, tuning, even your style of playing. Laurence Canty looks at these vital accessories, explaining windings, gauges and materials, and offers a tip or two

It's hard to believe now, but there was a time in the bad old days when the only choice in strings was which brand. Today there are not only more brands – each one claiming some special formulation or manufacturing process which gives an extra something – but also an almost overwhelming choice of gauges (diameters) and finishes.

Originally there were flatwound strings, available in a standard gauge which would be considered very heavy indeed by today's standards. Life was simple, strings were changed when necessary (when they broke), actions were high, and the bass lacked definition and was lost in the mix.

Then along came John Entwistle with a bass solo on The Who's "My Generation" (1965) which was more *twang* than *boom*. Nothing has been the same since. He got together with British string maker Rotosound and developed the roundwound string, which they called Swing Bass. The roundwound bass string is now considered the norm.

The importance of strings in the history of bass is easily under-estimated. Without roundwound strings the contemporary styles and sounds would not exist – imagine Jaco Pastorius' fretless with flatwound strings, or Mark King and Marcus Miller attempting to slap on flatwounds. If you want to hear how bass sounds have changed,

—Strings—

listen to Motown records of the 1960s – great songs, great feel, great lines, but a sound that few of us would be happy with today. Obviously this is partly a result of primitive recording techniques, but remember "My Generation" was contemporary.

There are disadvantages to roundwounds. They give greater wear and tear to fingers, frets (and fingerboards on fretless), and they produce increased string noise. The response to these problems has been the development of various forms of smooth roundwounds – 'halfwounds', 'groundwounds', and so on. But despite the makers' claims, these processes always seem to affect the tone adversely and the strings lack brightness.

GAUGES

String gauges are expressed in fractions of an inch, so that .040, for example, means a string forty thousandths of an inch in diameter. Over the years, strings have got lighter. Whereas .050 to .110 (a set from G at .050in to E at .110in) was once normal, now .040 to .100 might be more typical, and slappers may well use .030 to .090. A more subtle change has been that the top strings tend to be lighter relative to the E and A. For example, a 'hybrid' set of standard and medium gauge strings might go .040 (G), .060 (D), .080 (A), and .100 (E). These new combinations were put together as a response to what players were already doing for themselves: creating sets from individual strings.

Choice of gauge is obviously a matter of personal preference, but remember that a heavier string does have a better tone with more tension and better definition. So unless you spend all your time slapping and playing ultra-fast solos, it's best to avoid the very light sets – use the heaviest string which is comfortable and doesn't restrict your playing. If you haven't already done so, try a 'hybrid' set, often a good compromise between sound and speed for most types of playing.

One problem with all bass strings is a lack of definition on the lower strings. This occurs especially in high positions, because effectively you have a short fat string which cannot vibrate satisfactorily. Superwound's 'piano string design' – where only the core goes over the bridge – does improve the string's performance with a clearer tone, more sustain and better harmonics, although some players have found that they're more prone to break at the bridge.

For headless basses, the double-ball-end sets of the Bass Centre's

Different strings do different things. Designs change as new playing styles evolve, so you should experiment with various brands and gauges to find the best for you

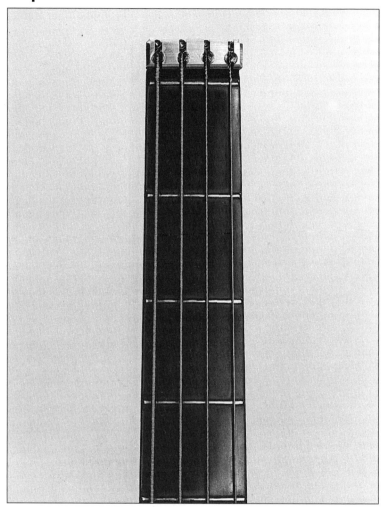

Headless basses necessitated development of double-ball-end strings

Elites have a similar effect with tapered windings at the bridge, a feature which has been included in all their Bs (and optional in Es).

A more recent development has been the introduction of nickel strings as an alternative to stainless steel. In theory, the nickels have less initial brightness but retain their original tone for longer. We haven't found that there is necessarily such a clear distinction, but steel strings seem to give a sound that more players like.

TIPS

Finally, a few tips for getting the most from a set of strings. When you're putting a new set on the bass, begin by trimming off the excess with wirecutters – but check there's enough left (about 10cm) to go around the machinehead. Then wrap as much as you can by hand around the machinehead, with the final turn at the bottom – this will help prevent the string from vibrating on the other side of the nut.

Then, while gripping the string between thumb and finger, run down the length of the string to the bridge to 'untwist' it. Now tune the string normally, then pull it away from the body to stretch it, and retune. Repeat this process until stretching doesn't affect the tuning. The string should now stay in tune.

Another useful tip is to tune your bass in the same position as you're going to play it – supported by a strap, or not, as the case may be – as any change of tension can affect the tuning. And always tune up, not down, to the right pitch, to avoid string slippage. Mute the strings you're not tuning so they don't resonate. Once the whole set has been put on, untwisted, stretched and tuned, it's time to check the intonation – see **PROBLEM SOLVING**.

If the budget won't cover a nice new set of strings, and an

Hand-wrapping new strings around the machinehead, with final turn at bottom

important gig is looming, there is a temporary solution: put the old set in a saucepan of water – make sure you take them off the bass first – and give them a quick boil. This will remove grime and give them a short reprieve (as well as making tasty soup). Some experts at this technique recommend adding vinegar or (a little) washing-up liquid to the recipe. Make sure the strings are dry before putting them back on – perhaps a couple of minutes in the oven, but definitely *not* the microwave.

STRING SURVEY

There's such an enormous variety of bass strings available that we're sure a little rationalisation by the makers would help – it might even cut costs and prices. There are roundwound, flatwound and in-between halfwounds or groundwounds. There are light, medium-light, medium, standard and heavy gauges, which often vary in size from one brand to another, there are nickel strings and stainless steel strings...

Making Music carried out a blindfold test with 12 leading sets of standard bass strings at the end of 1994. We restricted our survey to medium gauge (around .040, .060, .080, .100) roundwounds – surely the most popular variety. We know it's difficult for individual bassists to compare strings: when you replace a set after weeks or months, how can you compare the new set with the old? Even the same brand varies; and how do you rate a string's durability, which also depends on how you play, how often, and for how long? Consequently we concentrated on how strings compared when new.

A representative cross-section of bassists, plus one bass maker/repairer, was assembled, and strings compared to a reference or control set. The full results of the test can be seen in the January 1995 issue of *Making Music*, but, in brief, among the panel's favourites were the following:

MAXIMA GOLD 2299 (£28.97)
An "excellent" high quality string, our survey said; "how bass strings should be".

DR LO-RIDERS MH45 (£23.99)
Bright, good string tension, with a full-bodied, "expensive" feel.

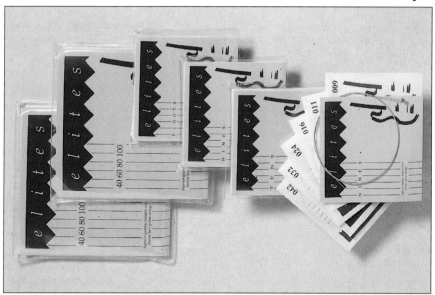

Perennial favourites among bass players: the Bass Centre's Elites

ELITES (£16.99)
Perennial favourites, solid, clean, with a lively fizz.

D'AQUISTO ROCK BOTTOMS 530 (£19.95)
Well-rounded and mellow, if a bit on the short side. A new name to most of the panellists, but one they said they'd remember in future.

ROTOSOUND SWING BASS (£16.75)
The original roundwound string brand, and still one of the best sounds, if slightly rattly (and liable to lose its cotton winding up top).

Of course, the bass string you eventually choose depends on the sound you want and on your bass – for instance, if your bass guitar has a bright sound anyway, then a warmer string might suit you best (and vice versa). If you can afford it, it's worth experimenting with brands and gauges until you find your perfect set.

AMPS, EFFECTS & ACCESSORIES

The spec and span of bass amps and speakers is laid out plainly by Andrew Bodnar, while Laurence Canty plugs in some effects and picks up some cases, tuners and stands

AMPS

Power is the key word in bass amplification, and it's the reason why the very best bass equipment can be expensive – pure power is costly to manufacture. Modern bass amps have to be able to handle a huge range of styles and sounds, from ultra low and power-consuming reggae and synth bass, through the gamut of pop, to the shattering high fidelity treble demanded by pull/slap players. Unlike guitarists for whom distortion, overload and other nasty noises may be quite desirable, bass players require the opposite. Overload is out. Plenty of power headroom is needed so that distortion doesn't occur at any volume.

It's as well to understand that the bass guitar is two things. As a rhythmic instrument, it makes deep and percussive sounds not at all unlike drums. As a stringed instrument, it can play notes and melodies in the same way as any other guitar. Deceptively simple, eh? Just as drummers are nearly always muscularly strong, which provides them with the energy to power their kits, so the bass player needs comparatively beefy amplification to power the loudspeakers which are, if you like, very advanced, remote controlled, motorised drum skins.

–Amps, Effects & Accessories–

Remember, the loudspeaker has to reproduce notes after the initial thud. So think of the bass guitar as a remote control unit; you play the strings and they provide the pickup with enough excitement to send tiny electrical impulses (a 'signal') to the amplifier to be boosted by enormous degrees, having been optimised and shaped by whatever facilities are available on the dashboard of the amp (tone controls, graphic EQ, volume and so on). The resulting high power signal is connected to the loudspeaker which is the mechanical part (the drum skin) that moves the air... and presto, bass sounds will begin to emerge.

Michael Anthony's Ampeg rig: a slight PA influence?

PA INFLUENCE

During the 1950s when the bass guitar was created, amplifier companies weren't entirely sure about, or interested in, catering for a sound they'd never heard before. Previously, the world had heard bass as an indistinct thud somewhere in the background. Luckily for the bass player the world has turned many times since, and bass amplifier technology and design have, in most respects, come a long way too, aided by the evolution of multi-kilowatt PA systems.

Modern PAs have clearly influenced today's larger bass rigs. Look at those separate power amps and pre-amps that the pro bassist uses on-stage, leaving the fiddlable bits separate from the business end. They may also use bi-amping and crossovers, which split up the sound into blocks of frequencies to feed separately to multi-speaker set-ups. But many PA features have worked their way down to more modest bass amps and combos, like graphic and parametric tone controls which give us more access to tonal variation than the usual bass and treble knobs, and compressors which 'smooth' the resulting sound. Two US amp makers, Ampeg and Acoustic, were notable in pioneering such features in the 1970s.

POWER

The three methods of popular playing – finger style, plectrum, and pull/slap – each impose heavy demands on the power section of an amp, and also on the loudspeaker. The continual impact of attack as thumb hammers E-string or plectrum strikes metal will place considerable and audible strain on any equipment not up to scratch. Amplifiers are generally power rated in watts (w). A modestly sized bass combo might be around 75w to 100w, and that should suffice for small intimate clubs or recording studios. At the other end of the spectrum, a multi-speaker system designed for concert hall or Wembley-sized stages would be rated at anything from 500w to 2000w and beyond – it depends how popular you are.

No matter what size of amp you're looking for, from tiny bedroom combo to massive rig, it's better to choose one with fewer facilities than one with pretty lights and hundreds of knobs that in practice you may never use. A worthwhile bass amp will be solidly built and probably weigh a lot, and will have facilities that are actually useful – for example a good quality, effective graphic EQ, so you can coax desirable sounds from your bass.

For the freelance pro bassist, the ideal is probably to own a high quality, small amp/combo for recording purposes, and a medium or splittable larger system for live work. Newcomers might be better looking for a tried-and-tested medium size system – it's worth seeking out a secondhand Ampeg, Carlsbro, Fender, Hartke, Peavey, Session,

SWR or Trace Elliot, and there are plenty more to choose from. Very small combos (say less than 50-60w) will give you a noise all right, but always at the expense of any kind of deep bass, and are only really of use for private practice.

It's probably worth spending a little more if you can on something bigger (say 75–100w) so there is sufficient power if you want to play with other people. There are some specialist headphone amps for bass, too, but the headphones usually object to such abuse. Avoid a colossal set-up unless you are assured of its use over a long period ahead. This kind of gear is specialist, very costly, expensive to move about, and doesn't work properly within small confines.

SPEAKERS

Loudspeakers come in various diameters (usually 8in, 10in, 12in, 15in and 18in) and each has its own characteristics and uses. Although modern loudspeakers (even relatively compact ones) can handle huge blasts of power compared to those of 20 or even ten years ago, several laws of physics have yet to be conquered: it still holds true that the

Hartke 3500 combo: 240w of portable power

bigger the enclosure that houses the loudspeakers, the deeper the sound will be.

A big enclosure will also respond more smoothly in the lower registers, especially when the strings are pulled or struck hard. This tends to be the case regardless of the type of enclosure, of which there are several, referred to as: 'sealed' (self explanatory); 'ported' – aka 'reflex' or 'vented' (a hole in the front with a tube or duct behind to resonate and improve the lowest notes); and 'horn-loaded' or 'folded bass horn/bin' (couples loudspeakers to the air in the room with an expanded tube which for practical reasons is folded up inside the box, again improving low end). These methods of enclosure design improve 'efficiency', which means getting more 'loudness' from the speaker in relation to a steady amplifier input.

Even so, loudspeaker size plays a critical role in shaping the sound of the bass. Eight-inch and 10in speakers sound punchy and respond more immediately, with a clearer treble but usually very little real bass. The 12in is a compromise between that and the 15in and 18in speakers – the only ones that really shift the air and give you wedges of deep, throbbing bass (though with a slightly less impressive treble end).

Naturally, there are ways around these shortcomings, and this is why there is such an abundance of enclosures and combinations available. One approach is to use multiple (say four or eight) 10in speakers in an enclosure. The combined area of air being moved is now quite large, but the 10in speakers continue to deliver their punchy response, so you have an enclosure which offers a very lively treble with good bass as well – ideal for pull/slap players and associated dance music.

Another course of action for, say, a finger-style reggae bassist, would be to combine two 18in speakers with two 10in speakers, which would culminate in a very deep, powerful, low bass end, along with sufficient clarity and roundness from the tens.

Combos too come with a wide array of speaker combinations, and here you must balance the (presumably) original intention of a combo – portability – against quality and range of sound. The smallest useful combos have a single 12in or 15in speaker, but a single speaker smaller than that is of little use to the bassist – though recent advances in speaker and enclosure technology (as demonstrated by, among others, Gallien-Krueger, Trace Elliot and SWR) have made it possible to achieve remarkable results from very compact combo units.

It's now possible, with a certain amount of common sense and much auditioning, to tailor your amps and enclosures specifically for your own requirements in ways undreamt of by bass players even a decade ago.

Matching amp power to speaker enclosures to avoid speaker overload is made easier if you add roughly a third of the amp power again – assuming the speakers are of decent quality. Thus a 100w amp should work cleanly enough into a 130w enclosure, a 300w amp into a 400w enclosure (or two 200w enclosures), and so on.

Finally, the matter of ohms. An ohm is a measure of electrical resistance, or impedance, but you needn't bother any further than the fact that the impedance in ohms of a speaker enclosure (usually inscribed on the back near the input socket) should never be less than the figure specified next to the output socket on the amp. Costly or irreparable amp damage can otherwise occur.

Note that, if you are powering more than one enclosure from a single amp output, it is the *total* impedance of your speaker set-up that is relevant – and this will be *more* or *less* than the impedance of the individual units, depending on whether they are connected in series or parallel. If you find this baffling, check the details with your local shop.

CHECK IT OUT

Despite the temptation to blast away, it's worthwhile auditioning new gear with the amp volume control not much beyond the half way mark, and with tone/graphic and effects switched to 'flat', or off. That way you'll be able to hear instantly how the amp and speakers are going to sound, and what sort of character they have. You'll also be able to gauge power handling abilities pretty accurately. If possible, try the amp or combo in a room similar in size to where you'll be using it. A well-matched system – amp and enclosure separates or combo – normally works with optimum efficiency around the half way mark, and tonal adjustments shouldn't need to be too extreme.

It's worth listening to the speakers not just straight on, but off to one side to ensure the sound spreads well. The less you find yourself having to fiddle with an amp set-up, the more closely will it be suited to your own sound. Beware of gimmicks. Instead, seek out sensibly designed controls that work for you. After all the claims and innovations have settled into mid-distance and the paint job is beginning to rub off, a good amp will still be a good amp.

Combinations of speaker enclosures allow very precise tailoring of desired sound

Rane's PE51 Parametric Equalizer: 20Hz-300Hz range specifically for bass guitar

BASS EFFECTS

Effects have been described as "inspirational" by one authority and as "talent boosters" by another. Although at first sight these views seem completely opposite, in fact the second is only a slightly cynical version of the first. Before parting with a fortune, you should remember that an effect may only get used five per cent of the time. It may be wiser to spend the money on a better bass or amp which you can use all the time.

Having said that, I still find that the effect with the best mileage per gallon is the Boss Octaver OC-2 (around £65). Boss seem unaware of its bass application – it's only recommended for guitar in their booklet. It can generate notes one and/or two octaves below the one played – it can't cope with more than one note, but then, can you? More than one note confuses the poor gadget. For bass, turn off the second octave, set the first at one o'clock, and the direct level at three o'clock. It adds weight (with no wait) to any line, creating a bass-guitar-doubled-with-synth-bass sound – and is cheaper than a five-string. Use it as far as low B (second fret on the A-string). The depth is very impressive, and with a fretless it's great for Pino Palladino impressions.

In comparison, all other effects are expensive in relation to their usefulness. But our next choices would be a delay, and a chorus. Which one is more important depends on the sort of player you are. A solo will generally need a touch of reverb to bring it to life whereas 'normal' bass playing usually requires a dry sound for maximum definition in the mix. Again, fretless bass benefits especially on high melodic lines. Perhaps as a response to the grunge boom, Boss produced their first Bass Overdrive pedal, the ODB-3 (£75), in 1994.

A chorus supposedly simulates the sound of several instruments playing in unison. If you plug into one, I don't think you'll fool anyone, but it is an attractive effect. Using the right amount is important – too little and it's lost, too much and it swamps the sound. One problem can be a loss of bass response, but any chorus pedal designed specifically for bass should avoid that problem.

There are advantages in having separate pedals: you don't have to buy them all at once; if one breaks down the others still function; and you can upgrade in easy stages. But it is more convenient and flexible to have a programmable multi-effect unit, provided it has the necessary octave, delay, chorus, compression and equalisation. These enable the bassist to set up many different combinations and settings of effects and then recall them with a foot-controller.

For instance, the ART Nightbass SE has 400 programmable memories (399 more than the average bassist) and costs £849 with another £249 required for the foot controller. If you can get by with only

Bass EQ and flanger units from Boss; the range now includes a bass overdriver

128 memories then the Peavey Bassfex is a mere £499 plus £140 for the foot controller. An additional possibility with these units is to exploit their bi-amping facility. Send the low end to one amp (with maybe 12in or 15in speaker/s) and the mid and high frequencies to another amp with smaller speakers. A crossover would serve the same function, of course, but without providing any effects.

ACCESSORIES

Given a bass, an amp and the necessary leads, what other items should the modern bassist possess?

GIG BAG

First, a gig bag – or something more sturdy than a bin liner in which to carry the bass. Many players still assume that a hard case is necessary but most pro players use soft padded gig bags (£25-60+) which have the obvious advantages of being lighter and smaller. Whether you're on foot, in a car, bus or train, they're easier to handle and in normal circumstances give sufficient protection (although note that buying a very cheap one is often a false economy, as it won't offer enough protection, and will probably fall apart before long). If your bass is going to travel in the back of a truck then you'll need a proper flightcase as well.

GUITAR STAND

You can survive without a guitar stand but it does provide a safe resting place for your pride and joy and could easily pay for itself in prevented accidents. I've used several types over the last lew years but the best is my current choice – the Quik-Lok (about £18). It's available in black, white or red and is very stable and compact – and it folds up even smaller so it's handy for transporting and using on gigs. The more expensive Nanyo Catch-O-Matic is well worth a look too.

TUNER

Every band should have one – shared if necessary – even if it's just to avoid disputes. However, it's not a good idea to rely 100 per cent on a tuner and never learn to tune by ear. A chromatic tuner will enable you to check every fret when adjusting the intonation (see **PROBLEM SOLVING**), and will usually select the right note automatically, provided

It's in the bag – the hipper gigster's bass

you're within half a semitone. It can also be left plugged in-line (between instrument and amp), so a quick tune between songs is easy. Cheaper tuners start from around £15. Even more basic is a tuning fork. The shiny black ones made by John Walker are the best, cost about a fiver, don't need batteries, and fit in your pocket. Make sure you get one marked A440 – concert pitch – which is what we're all supposed to tune to.

GIG CASE

Rather than a plastic carrier bag, choose something substantial to store and carry all your bits and bobs – the leads, stand, spare strings, fuses, strap, tools, batteries and so on. If they have a permanent home you're less likely to forget to take them (unless you forget the case), because all you have to do is remember how many items you should have: bass, amp, effects and case. So if you have less than four you've forgotten something – even in post-gig trauma that calculation should be easy. My suggestion is a drum case of suitable size. You could even stencil your name on it and pretend you're a star.

BASS
HISTORY

The electric bass guitar was born over 40 years ago. Tony Bacon traces the instrument's past, from Fender to Steinberger, and considers its present and future among MIDI and samples

Leo Fender must have been a time traveller. How else do you explain the fact that a non-musician invented the bass guitar in 1951, and got it virtually all right, first time? Fender, a Californian radio repairman turned amp and guitar maker, invented the bass guitar at a time when the bassist in a band would be stuck with a bulky, cumbersome, and often barely audible instrument, the double bass – what Leo called 'the doghouse'. He figured that bass players would welcome a louder, more portable instrument that offered precise pitching of notes.

So in 1951 he gave them the aptly-named Fender Precision Bass, for $195.50. Many of its features were based on Fender's already successful and equally astounding solid six-string electric guitar, the Telecaster. And three years after the Precision, he came up with the Stratocaster. Not bad going, really.

The Fender Precision was an ash-bodied, maple-necked bass, its four strings tuned EADG like the double bass and their sound amplified by a simple four-pole pickup controlled by a knob each for volume and tone. In 1957, Leo restyled the Precision, making it look much as it still does today: Strat-like headstock, sculpted body, and that distinctive split pickup. Pioneering early Precision users included jazz player Monk

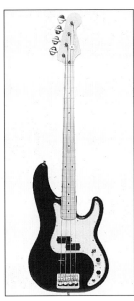

Left: the late Leo Fender, wiring his way into history; right: legendary Precision

Montgomery of the Lionel Hampton Band, along with a Stetson-full of country players who constituted a large percentage of Fender's customers at the time. The Precision is of course still widely used, and the design has been much copied by other bass makers.

And so Fender's new electric bass brought the bassist back into earshot and presented the willing player with a sudden wealth of musical potential. Leo's ability to get so much right on his original, innovative design remains an astounding feat – and most bass makers recognise this achievement by incorporating Fender's features to some degree on nearly all the bass guitars made today.

ALTERNATIVES

Fender's second bass design, the Jazz Bass, was introduced in 1960, distinguished by an offset body shape akin to its contemporary, the Jazzmaster six-string. It also differed in the narrow string spacing at the nut and the twin pickup arrangement which gave wider tonal variation via three knobs (volume per pickup, and overall tone). In fact, a second bar-type pickup is now a common addition to single-coil-style basses to give them extra whack. Popularisers of the Jazz Bass in the 1970s included Jaco Pastorius and, in the 1980s – when the instrument was rediscovered as a good one for the fashionable slapping style – session bassist Marcus Miller.

Talk to six-string guitarists for long about Fender and they'll ask: "What about Gibson?" Fender's old rivals have not done so well with basses: the company introduced their first electric four-string in 1953, the original 'violin bass'. This design was copied by the German maker Hofner and ensured widespread popularity when The Beatles' Paul McCartney toured extensively with a Hofner violin bass in the 1960s. Gibson's brief bass popularity came about toward the end of the 1960s when Jack Bruce of Cream used an EB3, a double-cutaway twin-pickup bass. But this accomplished six-string maker never appeared to realise that basses were not merely four-string versions of guitars: Gibson's humbucker-equipped basses sounded muddy, not helped by their medium-scale necks, and they've never been viewed as serious bass contenders, despite recent relaunches of attractive Les Paul basses, and own-brand Epiphone copies.

Rickenbacker basses first appeared in 1957 with the debut of their 4000 model, but proved popular when used by players like Paul McCartney in the late 1960s, Chris Squire of Yes in the 1970s, and later in that decade, Bruce Foxton of The Jam. They are renowned for a clanky, toppy sound, though this is often due as much to the player's style and amplification as it is to the fragile Ricky.

ACTIVATION

Active circuitry, which offers increased tonal range from an on-board pre-amp, is older than you might think: the first bass to feature such a circuit was the Burns TR2 launched by supreme British guitar maker Jim Burns in 1963 and featuring an on-board nine volt battery to power an active volume, bass and treble circuit for this semi solid bass.

But it wasn't until later that active electronics were made more widely available, originally through the work of American company Alembic, formed in the late 1960s as a workshop to provide technical support for the Grateful Dead's bizarre equipment requirements. Luthier Rick Turner joined Alembic and the company began to produce exclusive, high-quality and expensive basses made from exotic woods and with brass fittings – some even had twinkling LEDs for position

RD Artist active: pioneering product of Gibson's late '70s collaboration with Moog

markers. Stanley Clarke was among the elite of 1970s bassists able to afford Alembic's top-notch basses, and the company was among the first to establish the idea of the specialist bass guitar maker.

Leo Fender started making basses for the new Music Man company in 1972 after selling Fender to CBS in 1965, and an early product was the still-popular Stingray bass which did much to popularise active electronics and further the already glowing reputation of Leo Fender among bassists. For the last decade before his death in 1991, Leo headed up his own G&L company, which continues to make excellent, if rarely seen basses.

FIVES, SIXES & FRETLESS

The first five-string bass was the weird Fender V, launched in 1965 with an extra high C-string above the normal EADG, a small body, and, as it turned out, a short lifespan. In the 1980s, 'proper' five-string basses began to emerge, from up-market makers like Ken Smith and Alembic, with an extra low B-string below the E – primarily as the result of bassists wishing to emulate low synth-bass parts. This led one British make, Overwater, to make their C-bass in 1985, a low-tuned four-string (C, F, B*b*, E*b*). Now fives are everywhere.

Leo Fender launched the first six-string bass, the Bass VI, in 1962. In fact it was really a guitar, but tuned an octave lower than normal; players largely ignored it. It wasn't until the mid-late Eighties that wide-necked six-string basses appeared, and these became popular with some session players, such as American Anthony Jackson with his Fodera six-string. Where the original Fender VI was a low-tuned guitar, six-string basses now are clearly basses with extra strings (a B below and a C above the normal four), balancing the awkwardness of the wide neck with the advantage of an extended range of notes. For the truly adventurous bassist there's even a seven-string bass, with a high F above the C.

The first production fretless bass was made in 1965 by Ampeg – the AUB1: it had a semi-solid body with f-holes cut right through it, and featured a bridge-mounted transducer so that it had no visible pickup (an idea taken up in 1985 by the Japanese maker Bass Maniac). Fretless bass playing took off in the mid-1970s, helped by pioneering players like Ralphe Armstrong of John McLaughlin's Mahavishnu Orchestra, and Jaco Pastorius, who remains the bassist most clearly associated with the origins of fretless bass playing. Pastorius removed the frets himself from his Fender Jazz Bass. (See **WHY A FRETLESS?**)

WOODLESS AND HEADLESS

A lembic luthier Rick Turner and designer Geoff Gould produced the first graphite neck for a bass in 1977, and their patent was issued the following year when the two set up their Modulus Graphite company to exploit this rigid, non-warping material with high stiffness-to-weight ratio.

The world's first commercial, headless bass guitar, The Steinberger Bass, was launched in 1982, and was made almost entirely from graphite. The Steinberger was designed to diminish dead-spots (notes which fail to ring clear) and to enhance sustain and clarity of tone. The first examples of this tiny New York-made bass to arrive in the UK cost a staggering £950, but nonetheless the bizarre looking instrument caught on and within a year or two, every bassist with a record company advance seemed to be playing the diminutive black bass, and every guitar maker seemed to be turning out headless basses.

In Britain the first maker to build a bass using graphite was Rob Green, whose classy Status basses went into full production in 1983. This original Status Series II bass has a graphite core and wooden 'wings', and is still in production, while some later Status basses effectively use an all-graphite construction.

Budget-priced basses from Japan and other eastern countries

began to modify the player's idea of value for money in the 1980s, and in the UK it was the Westone Thunder which came to characterise this improvement in quality for price. Here was a budget instrument that was playable and well put together, had a long-scale neck and an active option, and offered good, usable sounds. If the Thunder helped establish such valuable precedents, other budget-bass builders soon joined in, and the budget Squier and Japanese-built Fender 're-issues' of original Precision and Jazz designs have added to the reputation of cheaper eastern-made basses.

In the early Nineties, £100 Indian-made Encores – although not original in design – brought a new standard in ultra-budget electric basses. In most recent times, the budget manufacturing base seems to be shifting from Japan and Korea to India, China and Mexico.

AND THEN...

The idea of using MIDI to help bassists play synthesised and sampled sounds from a bass guitar 'controller' is something that's been kicking about for quite a few years. Japanese high-tech company Roland launched their G77/GR77B MIDI bass system in 1985. The bassist had to use the supplied controller, feeding either the preset and edited sounds of the control unit, or the sounds of an external synth/sampler. In the late Eighties, Australian Steve Chick, of Bass Technology in Sydney, designed the MB4 MIDI Bass, which used a system where each fret provided a switch to tell the synth which note was being played. British bass specialist Wal, founded by the late Ian Waller in the 1970s, incorporated the MIDI Bass system into a heavily modified Wal bass guitar, involving remodelling of the neck to take the system's resistors and wiring.

More recently, Peavey Electronics in the US have taken the same basic design and developed it (employing Steve Chick himself to do so) – the result is the Cyberbass (formerly the Midibase), which is more user-friendly, and more sensitive to bass-playing subtleties like pitch bends and slides than its predecessor.

For some players, developments like this - and new devices like Korg's G5 and Roland's V system - can create sounds from the bass that Leo Fender couldn't have dreamt of in 1951. The point is the bass guitar has managed to adapt and react to player's needs over its 40-odd year history. It's capable of modernising if necessary; it still thrives in its

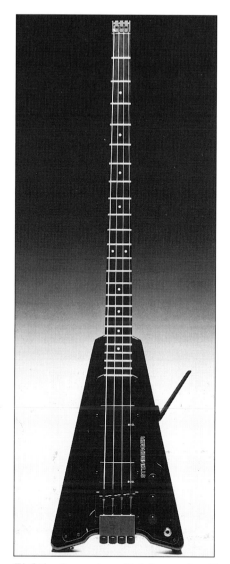

Eighties Innovators: Steinberger headless (L); early Roland bass synth controller

almost original form for those who believe in a straight, back-to-basics approach; and it's comfortable with all permutations between the two.

In short, the bass guitar looks set to continue as an irreplaceable component of modern music making for some time to come.

LISTENING OUT

Tony Bacon and Paul Quinn present a list
of best bassists' breathtaking basslines

The idea of this section is to suggest some alternative listening. It's set out in an A-Z of good, different and in some cases brilliant bass players. This is a personal selection across all types of music, and the entries are not meant to be complete discographies. We hope you enjoy what you hear; you might even absorb some inspiration along the way.

Individual tracks are shown in "double quotes"; albums are in 'single quotes'. Any solo records issued under the artist's own name are listed first; work for others follows, with the name of the act first in **bold type**, then the record titles; different acts are separated by semi-colons. The date following the record title is the year of release; compilations note a range of dates (eg *73-80*) showing the period covered.

RALPHE ARMSTRONG
Mahavishnu Orchestra 'Apocalypse' *74*, 'Visions Of The Emerald Beyond' *75*

VICTOR BAILEY
'Bottoms Up' *89*; **Weather Report** 'Procession' *83*, 'Domino Theory' *84*, 'This Is This' *85*

ASTON BARRETT
Burning Spear 'Marcus Garvey' *76*; **Bob Marley & The Wailers** 'Legend' *73-80* collection

MARK 'BEDDERS' BEDFORD
Madness 'Divine Madness' *92* best of

−Listening Out−

ROBERT 'KOOL' BELL
Kool & The Gang 'Twice As Kool – The Hits Of' *73-83 collection*

JEFF BERLIN
'Champion', 'Pump It' *80s solo albums*; **Bruford** 'Gradually Going Tornado' *80*

ANDREW BODNAR
Elvis Costello "Watching The Detectives" *77*; **Graham Parker & The Rumour** 'Squeezing Out Sparks' *79*, 'Mona Lisa's Sister' *88*, 'Struck By Lightning' *91*

TIM BOGERT
'Progressions' *81*; **Beck Bogert & Appice** 'BB&A' *73*; **Vanilla Fudge** 'VF' *67*, 'The Beat Goes On' *68*

RAY BROWN
'A Ray Brown Three' *83*; **Dizzy Gillespie** 'DG 1946-49'; **Oscar Peterson** 'One O'Clock Jump' *53*; **Duke Ellington** 'This One's For Blanton' *72*

JACK BRUCE
'Songs For A Tailor' *69*, 'Harmony Row' *71*, 'Out Of The Storm' *74*, 'Willpower' *68-87 collection*, 'A Question Of Time' *90*; **Cream** 'Strange Brew – The Very Best Of Cream' *60s collection*

JEAN-JACQUES BURNEL
Stranglers 'Collection' *70s/80s best-of*

JACK CASADY
Jefferson Airplane '2400 Fulton Street' *mainly 60s collection*; **Jimi Hendrix** "1983" from 'Electric Ladyland' *68*

KIM CLARKE
Defunkt 'In America' *88*, 'Avoid The Funk' *80s collection*

STANLEY CLARKE
'Stanley Clarke' *74*, 'Schooldays' *76*, 'If This Bass Could Only Talk' *88*, 'The Collection' *73-88 best-of*; **Return To Forever** 'Hymn Of The Seventh Galaxy' *73*

74

ADAM CLAYTON
U2 'The Joshua Tree' *87*, 'Rattle & Hum' *88*, 'Achtung Baby' *91*

CAROL COLMAN
Kid Creole And The Coconuts 'Fresh Fruit In Foreign Places' *81*

Parliament 'Greatest Hits' *70s best-of*; **Deee-Lite** "Groove Is In The Heart" *90*

NEIL CORCORAN
Mother Earth 'Stoned Woman' *92*, 'The People Tree' *94*

BOOTSY COLLINS
'Stretching Out In Bootsy's Rubber Band' *75*, 'Bootsy? Player Of The Year' *78*; **James Brown** 'Sex Machine' *70*, 'Super Bad' *71*; **Funkadelic** 'Cosmic Slop' *73*, 'One Nation Under A Groove' *78*;

GLENN CORNICK
Jethro Tull 'Original Masters' *60s/70s collection*

RICK DANKO
The Band 'TB' *69*

KIM DEAL
Pixies 'Surfer Rosa' *88*, 'Trompe Le Monde' *91*; **Breeders** 'Pod' *90*

–Listening Out–

Chic/Sister Sledge 'Freak Out
– The Greatest Hits Of' *73-87
collection*
JOHN ENTWISTLE
The Who 'Live At Leeds' *70,*
'Who's Better, Who's Best'
60s / 70s collection
WILTON FELDER
Crusaders 'Street Life' **79**;
Steely Dan some tracks on
'Katy Lied' *75*; **Randy
Crawford** 'Now We May Begin'
80; **Jackson Browne** 'For
Everyman' *73*

GAIL ANN DORSEY
'Rude Blue' *92*
DUCK DUNN
Otis Redding 'Otis Blue' *65*;
Booker T and the MGs 'Best
Of' *mainly 60s collection*; **Sam
& Dave** 'Greatest Hits' *mainly
60s collection*
NATHAN EAST
Eric Clapton 'August' *86*, '24
Nights' *91*; **Kenny Loggins**
"Footloose" *84*; **Whitney
Houston** "Saving All My Love
For You" *85*; **Michael Jackson**
"I Just Can't Stop Loving You"
on 'Bad' *87*
BERNARD EDWARDS

FLEA
Red Hot Chilli Peppers
'Mother's Milk' *89*, 'Blood Sugar
Sex Magik' *92*, 'Out In LA' *94*

HERBIE FLOWERS
'A Little Potty' *80*; **Blue Mink** 'Best Of' *70-73 collection*; **David Bowie** 'Space Oddity' *69*; **Elton John** 'Madman Across The Water' *71*; **Lou Reed** "Walk On The Wild Side" *72*; **Sky** 'The Very Best Of' *79-84 collection*

DEREK FORBES
Simple Minds 'Sparkle In The Rain' *86*

MO FOSTER
'Bel Assis' *88*, 'Southern Reunion' *91*; **Jeff Beck** 'There And Back' *80*; **Gerry Rafferty** 'Night Owl' *79*; **Dennis Waterman** "I Could Be So Good For You" *80*; **Phil Collins** two tracks on 'Hello I Must Be Going' *82*; **Gil Evans** 'Take Me To The Sun' *91*

TOM FOWLER
Frank Zappa 'Roxy & Elsewhere' *74*, 'One Size Fits All' *75*

BRUCE FOXTON
The Jam 'Greatest Hits' *77-82 best of*

ANDY FRASER
Free 'The Free Story' *70s best-of*; 'All Right Now' *remixed 70s best-of*

TONY GAD
Aswad 'Renaissance' *80s best-of*

JOHN GIBLIN
Simple Minds 'Street Fighting Years' *89*; **Phil Collins** four tracks on 'Face Value' *81*; **Kate Bush** "Breathing" on 'Never For Ever' *80*; **Brand X** 'Is There Anything About' *82*

KIM GORDON
Sonic Youth 'Goo' *91*

BILLY GOULD
Faith No More 'Introduce Yourself' *87*; 'The Real Thing' *89*

LARRY GRAHAM
Sly & the Family Stone 'There's A Riot Going On' *71*, 'The Collection' *70s best-of*; **Graham Central Station** 'GCS' *74*

PAUL GRAY
The Damned 'The Best Of' *76-84 compilation*

RUTGER GUNNARSSON
Abba 'The Singles: The First Ten Years' *73-82 collection*

STU HAMM
'Radio Free Albemuth' *88*, 'Kings Of Sleep' *89*, 'The Urge' *91*

JET HARRIS
The Shadows "Jet Black", "Kon-Tiki", "Nivram", "The Savage", "Wonderful Land" *60-62*

STEVE HARRIS
Iron Maiden 'Seventh Son Of A Seventh Son' *88*, 'No Prayer For The Dying' *90*

JONAS HELLBORG
'The Word' *91*

COLIN HODGKINSON
Back Door 'BD' *73*

DAVID HOOD
Muscle Shoals Rhythm Section, at Alabama studio of same name; *60s* tracks include **Percy Sledge** "When A Man Loves A Woman"; **Wilson Pickett** "Mustang Sally";

–Listening Out–

Aretha Franklin "I Never Loved A Man"; **Arthur Conley** "Sweet Soul Music"

PETER HOOK
Joy Division 'Unknown

Pleasures' *80*; **New Order** 'Best Of' *94*

ASHLEY HUTCHINGS
Fairport Convention 'Liege And Lief' *69*

ANTHONY JACKSON
O'Jays 'For The Love Of Money' *73*; **Quincy Jones** 'Sounds And Stuff Like That' *78*; **Steely Dan** two tracks on 'Gaucho' *80*; **Chaka Khan** 'Naughty' *80*, 'What Cha Gonna Do For Me' *81*; **Paul Simon** most tracks on 'Hearts And Bones' *83*; **Michel Camilo Trio** 'Suntan' *86*; **Al Di Meola** 'Elegant Gypsy' *77*

JAMES JAMERSON
The supreme **Motown** bassist. It's not known for sure who played on which Motown tracks but our fave cuts for basslines include **The Four Tops** "I Can't Help Myself" *65*, "Reach Out" *66*, "Bernadette" *67*; **Stevie Wonder** "I Was Made To Love Her" *67*, "For Once In My Life" *68*; **The Supremes** "Stop In The Name Of Love" *65*, "You Keep Me Hanging On" *66*, "Honey Bee" *68*; **Marvin Gaye** "I Heard It Through The Grapevine" *69*; **The Jackson Five** "ABC" *70*, "Darling Dear" *71*; **The Isley Brothers** "This Old Heart of Mine" *66*

ALEX JAMES
Blur 'Parklife' *94*

JERRY JEMMOTT
Aretha Franklin 'Live At The

Fillmore' *71*; **Roberta Flack** "Killing Me Softly With His Song" *73*

ALPHONSO JOHNSON
'Spellbound' *77*; **Weather Report** most tracks on 'Black Market' *76*; **Phil Collins** five tracks on 'Face Value' *81*

LOUIS JOHNSON
The Brothers Johnson 'Look Out For Number One' *76*; **Michael Jackson** 'Off The Wall' *79*, 'Thriller' *82*; **Quincy Jones** 'The Dude' *81*

DARRYL JONES
Miles Davis 'Decoy' *84*, 'You're Under Arrest' *85*; **Sting** 'Dream Of The Blue Turtles' *85*, "Bring On The Night" *86*; **Rolling Stones** 'Voodoo Lounge' 94

JOHN PAUL JONES
Led Zeppelin 'Remasters' *69-76 best-of*

PERCY JONES
'Cape Catastrophe' *89*; Brand X 'Moroccan Roll' *77, 'Masques' 78*

MICK KARN
Japan 'Tin Drum' *81*

CAROL KAYE
Beach Boys "Help Me Rhonda" *65*, "Good Vibrations" *66* "Wouldn't It Be Nice" *66*; **Joe Cocker** "Feeling Alright" *68*; **Glen Campbell** "Wichita Lineman" *69*; **Barbra Streisand** "The Way We Were" *73*

BAGHITI KHUMALO
Paul Simon five tracks on

'Graceland' *86*, four on 'Rhythm Of The Saints' *90*

MARK KING
'Influences' *84*; **Level 42** 'World Machine' *85*, 'Physical Presence' *85*, 'Guaranteed' *91*

ABRAHAM LABORIEL
Lee Ritenour 'Captain's Journey' *78*; **Joe Sample** 'Carmel' *79*; **Randy Crawford** 'Now We May Begin' *80*, 'Secret Combination' *81*; **Crusaders** "Soul Shadows" on 'Rhapsody & Blues' *80*; **Donald Fagen** "New Frontier" on 'Nightfly' *82*; **Tania Maria** 'Love Explosion' *84*; **Dave Grusin/Lee Ritenour** 'Harlequin' *85*

RICK LAIRD
'Soft Focus' *77*; **Mahavishnu Orchestra** 'Inner Mounting Flame' *71*, 'Birds Of Fire' *73*

BILL LASWELL
'Hear No Evil' *88*

GEDDY LEE
Rush 'Hold Your Fire' *87*, 'Show Of Hands' *88*, 'Roll The Bones' *91*

WILL LEE
Spyro Gyra 'Morning Dance' *78*; **Donald Fagen** "Walk Between The Raindrops" on 'Nightfly' *82*, **The Brecker Brothers** 'TBB' *75*; **Bee Gees** 'ESP' *87*; **Carly Simon** "Coming Around Again" *87*

PHIL LESH
With **Ned Lagin** 'Seastones' *75*; **Grateful Dead** 'Live Dead' *69*, 'Blues For Allah' *75*, 'Dead Set' *81*

Tony Levin

TONY LEVIN
Paul Simon tracks on 'Still Crazy After All These Years' *75*; **Peter Gabriel** 'So' *86,* 'Secret World Live' *94*; **Robert Fripp** 'Exposure' *79*; **King Crimson** 'Discipline' *81*; **Lou Reed** 'Berlin' 73

PHIL LYNOTT
Thin Lizzy 'Dedication – The Very Best Of' *73-80 collection*

MICHAEL MANRING
'Unusual Weather' *86,* 'Toward The Center Of The Night' *89,* 'Drastic Measures' *91*

PAUL McCARTNEY
The Beatles 'Rubber Soul' *65,* 'Revolver' *66,* "Rain" "Paperback Writer" *66,* 'Sgt Pepper' *67,* 'The Beatles' *68*; **Wings** "Silly Love Songs" *76*

DUFF McKAGAN
Guns N' Roses 'Appetite For Destruction' *87,* 'Use Your Illusion I & II' *91*

MARCUS MILLER
'Suddenly' *83,* 'Marcus Miller' *84*; **Miles Davis** 'The Man With The Horn' *86,* 'Tutu' *86,* 'Amandla' *89*; **Donald Fagen** three tracks on 'Nightfly' *82*; **Was Not Was** some tracks on 'What Up Dog?' *88*

MICHAEL MILLS
REM 'Out Of Time' *91,* 'Best Of' *82-87 collection* 'Automatic For The People' *93,* 'Monster' *94*

MONK MONTGOMERY
Lionel Hampton 'The Complete Paris Sessions' *53*

Michael Mills

COLIN MOULDING
XTC 'Beeswax/Waxworks' *77-82 singles collection* ; 'Skylarking' *86,* 'Oranges & Lemons' *89*

NEIL MURRAY
Whitesnake 'Ready & Willing' *80,* 'Live In The Heart Of The City' *80,* '1987' *87*; **Black Sabbath** 'Tyr' *90*

CHRIS NOVOSELIC
Nirvana 'Nevermind' *91*; 'In Utero' *93*

PINO PALLADINO
Paul Young 'No Parlez' *83*, 'Other Voices *90*; **Joan Armatrading** 'The Shouting Stage' *88*; **Julia Fordham** some tracks on 'Swept' *91*; **Phil Collins** two tracks on 'But Seriously...' *89*; **Oleta Adams** 'Circle Of One' *90*

JACO PASTORIUS
'Jaco Pastorius' *76*, 'Word Of Mouth' *81*, 'Twins' *82*; **Weather Report** three tracks on 'Black Market' *76*, 'Heavy Weather' *77*, 'Night Passage' *80*, '8:30' *81*, 'Collection' *77-81 best-of*; **Pat Metheny** 'Bright Sized Life' *76*; **Joni Mitchell** 'Hejira' *76*, 'Don Juan's Reckless Daughter' *77*, 'Mingus' *79*, 'Shadows & Light'

80; **Michel Colombier** 'Dreamland' *79*; **Flora Purim** "Las Olas" on 'Everyday, Everynight' *78*; **Herbie Hancock** "4am" on 'Mr Hands' *81*

JOHN PATITUCCI
'John Patitucci' *88*, 'On The Corner' *89*, 'Sketchbook' *90*; **Chick Corea Electrik Band** 'CCEB' *87*, 'Inside Out' *90*; **Manhattan Transfer** 'Vocalese' *85*; **Was Not Was** some tracks on 'What Up Dog?' *88*

DAVE PEGG
Fairport Convention 'Full House' *70*, 'Farewell, Farewell', 'Red & Gold' *88*, 'The Five Seasons' *91*; **Jethro Tull** 'Crest Of A Knave' *87*, 'Catfish Rising' *91*

GEORGE PORTER
The Meters 'Best Of' *72-75 collection*

GUY PRATT
Madonna "Like A Prayer" *89*; **Pink Floyd** 'Delicate Sound Of Thunder' *88*; **Robbie Robertson** some tracks on 'Storyville'; **Bryan Ferry** "Kiss And Tell" *88*

ROCCO PRESTIA
Tower Of Power 'Bump City' *72*, 'Tower Of Power' *73*, 'Back To Oakland' *74*, 'Power' *87*

CARL RADLE
Leon Russell 'And The Shelter People' *71*, 'Carney' *72*; **Eric Clapton** 'EC' *70*, '461 Ocean Boulevard' *74*

CHUCK RAINEY
'Chuck Rainey Coalition' *72*; **King Curtis** 'Live At Smalls Paradise' *66*; **Crusaders** 'Crusaders' *72*; **Steely Dan** most of 'Aja' *77*, some of 'Gaucho' *80*; **Donald Fagen** "Green Flower Street" on 'Nightfly' *82*

ANDY ROURKE
The Smiths 'Meat Is Murder' *85*, 'The Queen Is Dead' *86*

PAUL RYDER
Happy Mondays 'Pills 'N' Thrills And Bellyaches' *90*

BILLY SHEEHAN
David Lee Roth 'Eat 'Em And Smile' *86*, 'Skyscraper' *88*; **Mr Big** 'Mr Big' *89*, 'Lean Into It" *91*

MUZZ SKILLINGS
Living Colour 'Vivid' *88*, 'Time's Up' *90*

LEE SKLAR
James Taylor 'Mud Slide Slim' *71*; **Jackson Browne** 'Running On Empty' *78*

ALAN SPENNER
Roxy Music 'Flesh & Blood' *80*; **Joe Cocker** 'Live In LA' *76*;

ROBBIE SHAKESPEARE
Burning Spear 'Marcus Garvey' *76*; **Grace Jones** 'Living My Life' *82*; **Chakademus & Pliers** 'Tease Me' *93*

Grease Band 'GB' *71*; **Steve Winwood** 'SW' *77*

CHRIS SQUIRE
'Fish Out Of Water' *75*; **Yes** 'The Yes Album' *71*, 'Fragile' *71*

–Listening Out–

TM STEVENS
Narada Michael Walden "I Shoulda Loved Ya" *82*

BRUCE THOMAS
Elvis Costello & The Attractions 'This Year's Model' *78*

STING
'Nothing Like The Sun' *87* 'The Soul Cages' *91*; **The Police** 'Every Breath You Take – The Singles' *70s/80s collection*

JAMAALADEEN TACUMA
'Renaissance Man' *84*; **Ornette Coleman's Prime Time** 'Dancing In Your Head' *76*

BILLY TALBOT
Neil Young 'After The Goldrush' *70*, 'Zuma' *75*, 'Weld' *91*; **Nils Lofgren** 'Cry Tough' *76*; Crazy Horse 'CH' *71*

ALAN THOMSON
John Martyn some tracks on 'Cooltide' *91*; **Julia Fordham** some tracks on 'Swept' *91*

MICHAEL VISCEGLIA
Suzanne Vega 'Solitude Standing' *87*, 'Days Of Open Hand' *90*

KLAUS VOORMAN
Carly Simon "You're So Vain" *72*; **John Lennon** 'Imagine' *71*

FREDDIE WASHINGTON
Patrice Rushen "Forget Me Nots" *82*

NORMAN WATT-ROY
Ian Dury 'New boots And Panties' 77, "Hit Me With Your Rhythm Stick" 78
NATHAN WATTS
Stevie Wonder 'Original Musiquarium' 72-81 collection
WILLIE WEEKS
Donny Hathaway 'Everything Is Everything' 70, 'Live' 72; Rickie Lee Jones 'RLJ' 79
JOHN WETTON
Family 'Fearless' 71, 'Bandstand' 72; King Crimson 'Larks' Tongues In Aspic' 73, 'Red' 74; Uriah Heep 'Return To Fantasy' 75
TINA WEYMOUTH
Talking Heads 'Talking Heads' 77, 'Remain In Light' 80, 'Naked' 88
VERDINE WHITE
Earth Wind & Fire 'I Am' 79
KEITH WILKINSON
Squeeze 'Frank' 89, 'A Round And A Bout' 90
DOUG WIMBISH
Grandmaster Flash "The Message" 82, "White Lines" 83; Tackhead 'Friendly As A Hand Grenade' 89, 'Strange Things' 91; Living Colour 'Stain' 93
JAH WOBBLE
'Rising Above Bedlam' 91; Public Image Ltd 'PiL' 78; Holger Czukay 'Movies' 79;
VICTOR WOOTEN
Bela Fleck & The Flecktones 'Flight Of The Cosmic Hippo' 91

Tina Weymouth

BILL WYMAN
Rolling Stones 'Hot Rocks' 64-71 collection
STUART ZENDER
Jamiroquai 'Emergency On Planet Earth' 92, 'Return Of The Space Cowboy' 94

THE BASS
MARKET

So, after all that, What Bass should you
actually buy? We round up your options

If you want information on the shiny new basses to be found in music
shops around the UK, then you're in the right place. Prices are
recommended retail, and include VAT at 17.5 per cent.

THE CHOSEN FEW
A personal selection of 20 leading basses
by Adrian Ashton

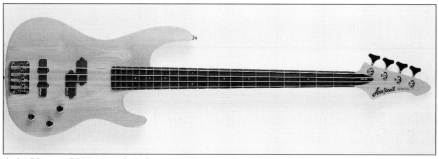

Aria Magna MAB20: a bright sounding, modern bass design (see over)

–The Bass Market–

ARIA MAGNA MAB20 (£349)

Korean made solid ash body bass with carved top and passive split & bar pickup layout. The 22-fret bolt-on maple neck and rosewood fingerboard is slim and comfortable with good access to the top frets courtesy of the deep cutaway on the lower horn. A bright sounding, modern design bass.

BASS COLLECTION SB315 (£629)

For the serious five-string player on a budget, the Japanese made SB315 is worth considering. A slim, lightweight solid alder body is bolted onto a 24-fret one-piece maple neck with 24-fret rosewood fingerboard. The twin bar pickups are powered by active circuitry, with bass, treble, volume and pan controls. A good low B sound and balanced string response result. Black Gotoh hardware and Elite strings as standard make this a recommended bass.

BC RICH IRONBIRD IB50 (£339)

If you're going for a bass that demands attention you might as well be completely outrageous, hence the choice of the Ironbird bass. If you don't mind the ply body, or single passive pickup, this is a bass for posing with. For under £500 nothing else comes close.

CARVIN LB70 (£775)

US-made bass with a long list of options. The LB70 has a poplar body and straight-through rock maple neck giving it a custom bass look. Active electronics feed two bar-style pick ups. The 24-fret fingerboard (ebony is available too) is easily accessed, as the lower body joins at the 22nd fret.

ELECTRIC WOOD WAL 6 STRING (£2138)

British handmade bass with solid mahogany core and exotic top (choice of paduak, wenge, American walnut or hydua). Bolt-on 21-fret neck with 24-fret option. Superb active EQ with quasi-parametric tone controls and DI output socket. The Wal is still regarded by many as one of the finest recording basses available.

ENCORE E83 (£149)

Despite a near 50 per cent price increase since its launch, the E83 is still amazing value. A solid ash chunk body (ie not ply nor solid but several solid pieces) is bolted to a maple and rosewood combination neck

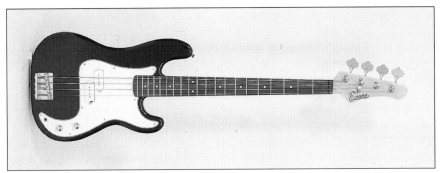

Encore E83B: a regular chart-topper

and fingerboard. A split type pickup with single volume and tone is sufficient to give several exceptional sounds at this price. More than a beginner's bass and justifiably a regular chart topper in the *Making Music Buyer's Bible*.

HOHNER B2B (£269)
A shameless Steinberger copy, the headless, bodyless Korean-made B2B offers all the advantages of ease of transport, light weight, accurate tuning and easy string changes – albeit with low-tech materials. Features include a maple body and bolt-on maple neck with 24-fret rosewood fingerboard. Two humbucking pickups with independent volumes and a single tone provide sufficient tonal variation.

IBANEZ SR800 (£699 including case)
Always a solid performer and now updated with the new vari-mid EQ, the Japanese 800 series boasts high specification. A resin cast body is mated to a 24-fret three-piece maple neck and rosewood fingerboard that's slim and comfortable to play. The EQ is fully active, with volume, pan, bass and treble on one concentric pot, and a semi-parametric system on a second. This gives excellent control over those vital mid-range areas, from deep twangy slap to growling fingerstyle funk.

MARTIN B65 (£2350 inc case)
Although better known for their acoustic six-strings, the B65 shows the same tradition and craftsmanship one would expect from this famed US manufacturer. A four-string dreadnought acoustic with solid spruce top and flame maple back and sides. The 23-fret neck is mahogany with an ebony fingerboard.

–The Bass Market–

MUSICMAN STERLING (£1069)
US-made, solid body (wood varies with colour choice) four-string only model, to supplement the consistently popular Stingray. Features birds eye maple, slim neck with maple or rosewood option fingerboard. Active single humbucker with bass, mid and treble plus single coil, series, parallel switch. Distinctive three-plus-one headstock layout.

OVATION ELITE B768 (£1699 INC CASE)
US-manufactured electro-acoustic bass with synthetic deep bowl back and solid spruce top (containing 11 'sound ports'). Mahogany neck with 24-fret rosewood fingerboard. Gold hardware, active EQ system and maple inlays make this an attractive and versatile instrument ready for your next 'unplugged' appearance.

PARKER FLY BASS
At the time of writing, this instrument exists purely as a concept. The proposal is to build a bass version of the very successful and uniquely-designed Fly guitar. An exoskeleton of composite material surrounds a softwood centre, resulting in a featherlight five pound weight. Both piezo and magnetic pickups are offered to give attack and warmth. Price when (if?) it appears is likely to be in the £2000 area.

PEAVEY CYBERBASS (£1850)
MIDI bass with 22-fret sensing fingerboard that sends note information to an outboard tone module (+£1099). Analogue sounds from two VFL active humbucking pickups can be blended with the synth sounds. Apart from a digital readout, the bass looks just like a standard instrument. A relaunched and improved version of the Midibase.

RICKENBACKER 4003 (£1159 INC CASE)
Few basses can call themselves 'classics', but the 4003 is one that can justify the title. A through-neck construction design with 20 frets on a rosewood fingerboard. Two passive single coil pickups can be linked, in stereo – each pickup has a separate output for that famous 'clanking' sound. This top-of-the-range US-made bass also features triangle inlays, binding and a bridge with string mutes.

SQUIER II PRECISION (£223)
The Fender bass range is simply huge, and to complicate matters further, production seems to change regularly from various factories.

Five and eight-string versions of Rickenbacker's renowned 4003 model

The new **Squier II Precision** is Korean, made with a ply body, maple neck, and choice of rosewood or maple fingerboards. A single passive Precision (split) pickup offers the usual tones. Competition is hot in this area but on prestige and resale the Fender connection wins hands down.

STATUS ENERGY (£699 inc gig bag)
Famous though Status is for exotic headless carbon fibre designs, the only graphite on the new UK-made Energy is two neck-reinforcing bars inside the headed maple bolt-on neck. Even the fingerboard is rosewood. Two new Hyperactive humbucking pickups sit on a solid mahogany or ash body, and feature volume, pan and single active tone control.

VESTER VB11 (£299)
Writ-inducing copies of Warwick basses with exotic looks for a remarkably reasonable price. The body is natural-finish body is maple, bolted to a five-piece maple neck with a 24-fret rosewood fingerboard. The twin humbucking pickups are active, with two volumes and a single tone control to keep costs down, though Gotoh machineheads and black hardware mean cost cutting is limited.

Warwick Corvette Proline: stylish German

WARWICK: CORVETTE PROLINE (£945 inc gig bag)

German-made basses with stylish body shapes, unlike anything else on the market. A maple/mahogany multi-laminate neck is bolted to a maple body with two active MEC bar style pickups, controlled by bass, treble, volume and pan pots. Plenty of EQ variations, new stain finishes, and high quality hardware – the Corvette is well worth testing out.

WASHBURN: XB800 (£499)

Four-string, bolt-on, 24-fret solid alder bass. Twin active humbucking pickups by Rob Green of Status give this bass a high quality sound, with a custom bass appearance helped by flamed sycamore top, bookmatched and available in transparent finishes. Small details such as gold hardware and offset dot fret markers complete a stylish package.

YAMAHA: TRB-5 (£999 inc case)

The latest models in Yamaha's TRB range now feature 24-fret bolt-on necks and a new EQ system which does away with the piezo bridge of the through-neck models (still in production). The TRB-5 is very versatile, with a solid low B sound with plenty of growl in it. A bass for those who like traditional sounds in a modern design. Twin humbuckers have volume, pan, bass and treble, as you'd expect, but also a new mid-range control which has three pre-set EQ settings; bypass, mid cut (for slap), and mid boost (for fingerstyle). All the EQ frequency centres are adjustable by internal trim pots and two boost/cut treble and bass switches.

BASS MODELS A-Z
Tony Bacon, Paul Ricketts & Paul Quinn
SURVEY THE MARKET

ALEMBIC

This Californian company virtually invented the idea of the specialist bass maker, and today offers a bevy of up-market, four to ten-string basses. The **Epic** (£895; five-string £995; six-string £1295) is their entry-level maple through-neck instrument; the **Essence** (£1195; five-string £1395; six-string £1595) has a double-cutaway offset body with twin hum-cancelling pickups feeding volume, pan, tone with Q switch, and two boost/cut treble and bass switches. The **Elan** (from £1795) is similar with two split pickups, 24-fret ebony fingerboard and a multitude of wood top construction and string choices. The **Spoiler**'s squat body with long body horns also features selected woods (£1695; five-string £1845). A couple of standard and deluxe signature models (£1845 to £1995; five-string £2495 to £2645) from well-known Alembic users are the **Mark King** bass, with a through-neck and mahogany body, and the **Stanley Clarke** bass, with a through-neck and cocobolo body. The **Europa** has a five-piece maple neck (from £1995), and the **Series I** (from £3695) two single-coil pickups either side of a hum-cancelling dummy coil, active electronics, outboard power supply and mono and stereo. Top of the range is the multi-laminated **Series II** (from £4595), blessed with pretty woods and a seemingly complex control layout. Nearly all custom options are available; it's not impossible to spend over £8000 on an Alembic if you're inclined.
Contact: The Bass Centre/House Music, 131 Wapping High Street, London E1 9NQ; Phone 0171 265 1567. .

APPLAUSE

This is a Korean-made range from **Kaman**, who own **Ovation**. The **AE140** (£415; fretless same price) is a bowl-back electro-acoustic bass with traditional body style and cutaway. Top is sitka spruce, bowl is synthetic, bridge walnut, neck mahogany and fingerboard rosewood (19 frets). Pickup is an under-saddle piezo job, with volume and tone knobs on the upper side of the bowl.
Contact: TE Distribution, Galliford Road, The Causeway, Essex CM9 7XD; Phone 01621 851851.

–The Bass Market–

ARIA

This far-eastern brand offers a confusing range of basses. The inevitable lookalike, the **Legend LPB10** (£179 fretless same price, left-handed add ten per cent), is followed by the basic **LJB10** (£189) with twin bar pickups; and the **LPB02** (£289) with split & bar pickups, active on/off and gold hardware. The **SLB 2** (£265) 22-fret, split & bar pickups, plus volume, tone and selector (there's an active **SLB 2A** £345, with active on/off and extra tone knob), and the **Integra Spirit** (£425) and **Standard** (£469) both have 24-frets, better body wood and split & bar pickups. The curved-top **Magna** series boasts the **MAB10** (£325) – 22-frets, split & bar pickups, two volumes and a tone; the **MAB10 Deluxe** (£389) with gold hardware; the **MAB20** (£349; five-string £369) with an ash body and scalloped cutaway, and the **MAB40** (£419) active version. The **AVB TN** six-string bass (£689) has maple through-neck construction, with twin active bar pickups; the **Steve Bailey Bass** comes in four (£1075), five (£1175) and six-string versions (£1275); the **Overwater** designed **AOW 1** (£769) has through-neck, active electronics, while the **AOW 2** (£569) has bolt-on neck, passive electronics. The **Feb Standard** (£599) is a electro-acoustic bass with piezo pickups and active battery powered pre-amp.
Contact: Aria (UK) Ltd, Unit 12, Heston Industrial Mall, Church Road, Heston, Middlesex TW5 0LD; Phone 0181 572 0033.

ASHBORY

Made in Britain, this unusual mini-bass (£499) has a 22in scale, a fretless board with 24 lined markers, toughened, coloured silicone rubber strings, and a piezo pickup in the bridge feeding volume, bass, treble, and active/passive switch. It actually does a remarkable impersonation of an upright bass, as well as delivering normal electric tones.
Contact: Blossom Reproductions, 2 Byron Road, Weybridge Trading Estate, Addlestone, Surrey KT15 2SZ; Phone 01923 859840.

BASS COLLECTION

From Japan, Bass Collection offers five models: the **SB311** (£469; fretless £469; five string £629) with 24 frets and split & bar pickups (five-string with twin bars) feeding volume, pan and two pickup tones; the similar **SB 411** (£769) with split pickups and active tones; the **SB511** (£999; left-handed £1099; five-string £1159) with better woods

Left: Aria MAB40; centre: Blade Tetra, and right: the Penta, from Blade

and hardware; and **SB611** (£1129; five string and six -string with twin pickups £1259 and £1599) using exotic woods plus gold hardware. Fretless version exists for all types for no extra cost.
Contact: The Bass Centre/House Music, 131 Wapping High Street, London E1 9NQ; Phone 0171 481 3350.

BC RICH
The idiosyncratic Korean-made Rich bass splits into two series: the **Gold 50** and **Diamond 100** series, all in a wide variety of colours. The **Gold**s (all £329, with laminated bodies) include: the **Warlock** (multiple cutaway body; split pickup; volume & tone), the **Mockingbird** (curved body with pointed horns), and **Ironbird** ('star-point' body), while the **Gunslinger** has a surprisingly conventional twin-cutaway body. The **Diamond Series** (all £469) has the same designs and names but with solid maple bodies and Hi-Power pickups.
Contact: Creative Distribution, Units 7&8 Anglia Way, Southwell Road West, Mansfield, Nottinghamshire NG18 4LP; Phone 01623 423330.

BLADE
Swiss-based American luthier Gary Levinson is the designer behind these two Japanese-made basses, promoted by the UK company

—The Bass Market—

formerly known as Blade-Eggle. The **Tetra** (£1199) has an ash body, maple neck, rosewood fingerboard, JHB-25 split coil pickups and gold hardware. The **Penta** is the five-string option (£1199).
Contact: British Guitar Factory, Bodmin Road, Coventry CV2 5DB; Phone 01203 602211.

CARVIN

This Californian maker's basic 24 fret, through-neck bass comes in four, five and six-string and fretless versions. The **LB20** (£599; all fretlesses same price) is the passive four-string, with Carvin's long-top-horn body shape in poplar, and twin bar humbuckers feeding a volume each and overall tone. The **LB70** is the active four, with volume, pan and active treble and bass controls; **LB75** (£729) the active five-string and **LB76** (£799) the active six. The **Bunny Brunel** designed five and six-string **BB70** (£740) and **BB75** (£799) differ by offering a wider, asymmetrical neck, a wider body and a longer upper horn.
Contact: ABC Music, Head Office, 55/58 Surbiton Road, Kingston, Surrey KT1 2HT; Phone 0181 974 5505.

CHARVEL

One model from this Japanese brand is imported to the UK. The lightweight **ATX Bass** (£899) has a maple top and neck and an acoustically chambered mahogany body (reducing traditional electro-acoustic feedback problems), and a Fishman transducer underneath the saddle feeding volume, bass, mid and treble controls.
Contact: John Hornby Skewes & Co Ltd, Salem House, Garforth, Leeds LS25 1PX; Phone 01132 865381.

CHERI

Korean-made brand, originally known as Chevy, but forced to change by makers of a certain American car... The **PB** (£299; left-handed £329) is the basic 20-fret, maple-body, split & bar pickup job; the **JB** (same price) has two bar pickups. The **SMB** (£375) is the pointy metal-oriented bass, 24 frets, split & bar pickups; while the **SLB4** (£395; **SLB4A** active, £495; **SLB5A** active five-string, £555) is the curvy, funky, up-market Cheri. The **N1B** is an electro-acoustic bass with active EMG pickup and cutaway.
Contact: DGC Distribution Ltd, Unit 20, Enterprise City, Green Lane, Spennymoor, Durham, County Durham DH1 4ED; Phone 01388 810300.

CRAFTER

Korean based manufacturer have one electro-acoustic bass available: the **BA-40E** (£269) with spruce top, mahogany neck, rosewood fingerboard and active controls.
Contact: M Hohner Ltd, Bedwas House Industrial Estate, Bedwas, Newport, Gwent NP1 8XQ; Phone 01222 887333.

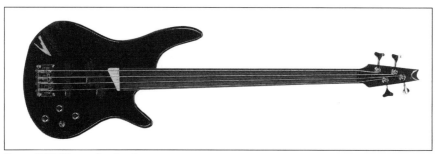

Dean DB91F passive fretless

DEAN

This Korean manufacturer offers four variations on their **DB91** bass format (£260), which has bolt-on maple neck, rosewood fingerboard and split & bar pickups; the **DB91L** left-hander and **DB91F** passive fretless (both £260); the **DB94** (£375) with 24-fret neck and active split & bar pickups; and **DB95** (£400) five-string featuring gold hardware.
Contact: Barnes and Mullins Ltd, 155 Grays Inn Road, London WC1X 8UF; Phone 0171 278 4631.

ENCORE

One of the most popular and cheapest basses about is the Indian-built **E83** (£143; left-hander same price; fretless £155), a basic 20-fret traditional bass guitar with split pickup, also available in fretless and left-handed versions. The **E84** (£165) differs by providing a split & bar pickup configuration and the **PK12** (£99) by having a pre-composite body and ebonised hardwood fingerboard.
Contact: John Hornby Skewes & Co Ltd, Salem House, Garforth, Leeds LS25 1PX; Phone 01132 865381.

EPIPHONE

Korean budget Gibsons, offering the **S700 Power Bass** (£259), a basic instrument with split & bar pickups feeding two volumes and a tone

control, a rosewood board with 20 frets and droopy headstock. The **Accu Bass** (£225) is similar with one humbucking split pickup and passive electronics. The 24 fret **EBM-4** (£365) has active electronics with cutaway, split & bar pickups, alder body, and bolt-on maple neck. The **EBM-5** (£389) is the five-string option, the **EBM-5 Custom** (£429) has a solid ash body and the Expert six-string (£645) has maple through-neck body and twin pickups. There's also the semi-acoustic **Rivoli** – 20 fret, 30in scale, one humbucker pickup (£399); and the **El Capitan Acoustic Electric** (£499) – piezo pickups, parametric EQ, Lo-z and Hi-z outputs and spruce top.
Contact: Rosetti Ltd, Tamdown Way, Springwood Industrial Estate, Braintree, Essex CM7 7QL; Phone: 01376 550033.

ESP
There are three basses from this Japanese brand currently available here: the jazzy **J-800** with 21-frets, twin bar pickups, ash body and maple rosewood neck (£1050); **J-Four** (£895) with 21-frets and alder body; and **J-Five** (£999) five-string version.
Contact: Selectron UK Ltd, Springhead Enterprise Park, Gravesend, Kent; Phone: 01474 320445.

FENDER
Fender's huge, ever-changing range has become slightly more streamlined of late – but is still confusing. Top of the four-string price range is the US-made **Stu Hamm Urge** bass (£1231), a sleek, 'modernised' take on the classic Precision, with 24 frets on a pau ferro board, alder body, two Custom Vintage J (bar) pickups, and split P-style in the middle; copious controls include active bass, treble, volume, pan, four-position rotary and three-position mini-switch. There's also a simpler Mexican-made **Urge** (£483) – rosewood board and no extra switches (£483). Fender's other signature bass model is the new **Roscoe Beck V** (£1266), a 22-fret 'modern vintage' design: pau ferro board, graphite reinforced neck, strings-thru-body or top-load bridge, and special five-string Dual J pickups. The **US Deluxe Series Precision** (£1007) also has graphite reinforcement for the 22-fret neck (maple or rosewood), and offers a three band active EQ, controlling P-style (split) pick-up and humbucker. The **US Jass Bass Deluxe** (£980) is much the same apart from two J pickups (**Jazz Deluxe V**, £1052). The **American Standard Jazz** (£839) has only 20 frets, and makes do with two plain vintage Jazz pickups (five-string £901), while the graphite-

Left: Fernandes BJ-1 in oil natural and see-thru purple; above: G&L ASAT

reinforced **American Standard Precision** comes in fretted (£789), fretless (£847) and left-handed (£891) versions. Then there's the **US Vintage Precision** (£892) and **Vintage Jazz** (£1003). Still with us? The **Precision Bass Lyte Standard** (£599) is a 22-fret down-sized body, split & bar pickups; the mahogany **Lyte Deluxe** has three-band EQ and gold hadware. The Japanese **Reissue** series comprises: **Reissue Precision** (£473) and **Jazz** (£496). Cheapest basses with Fender logos are from the Mexican series: **Standard Precision** (£387); **Standard Jazz** (£394); and **Precision Bass Special** (£457). Contact: **Arbiter Group plc, Wilberforce Rd, London NW9 6AX; Phone 0181 202 1199.**

FERNANDES

Two basses are offered by this mid-market Japanese brand: the jazzy-style **BJ-1** (£535), 21-fret with twin bar pickups, and the **BP-1** (£535), a trad 20-fretter with split & bar pickup configuration. Contact: **House Music, 131 Wapping High Street, London E1 9NQ; Phone 0171 481 3350.**.

G&L

US-made brand co-founded by Leo Fender, posthumously producing a selection of 21-fret basses: the traditional-looking **SB-1** (£730) and **LB-**

100 (£847) with split coil vintage pickup, and the jazzier **SB-2** (£825); the **Climax** (£1036) has a single humbucker, and two switches control the active/passive electronics and pre-amp. The **L-2000** (£1177) has two humbuckers and tri-tone active/passive electronics; the **ASAT** (£1177) is similar but has a single cutaway body and six piece construction neck. Top of the range is the **L-5000** five-string (£1399) with two EMG humbuckers feeding volume, pan, bass/treble controls.
Contact: Music & Audio Distribution Ltd, 10 Station Parade, Willesden Green, London NW2 4NH; Phone 0181 452 1009.

Gibson LPB-3 Les Paul Standard bass

GIBSON
The long established US maker has recently expanded its range of basses. The classic **Thunderbird** (*about* £1200 – note, recommended retail prices are not provided by Gibson's distributors) has 20 frets, mahogany through-neck and body 'wings', plus twin pickups feeding two volumes and tone. This has been joined by a new breed of models bearing the legendary **Les Paul** name (*around* £750-£1800). The **Standard** has 20 frets, mahogany body, maple top, mahogany neck, ebony fingerboard, twin 'TB Plus' pickups and Bartolini TCT active volume, bass, treble and blend controls. The **Special** is similar but with a different neck shape, the **Deluxe Plus**, Bartolini Bass HB twin pickups, active electronics, and both have five-string options.
Contact: Rosetti Ltd, Tamdown Way, Springwood Industrial Estate, Braintree, Essex CM7 7QL; Phone: 01376 550033.

GODIN

The unusual Canadian **Acoustibass** (£949; fretless same price) is built with a combination of electric and acoustic styles, with a spruce top on lime back/sides enclosing the Godin 'mechanical harp' (vibrating metal rods to improve resonance), plus long thumb-rest, ebony bridge with built-in LR Baggs piezo pickup, and a control plate near the top cutaway with sliders for volume plus active bass, mid and treble.
Contact: M Hohner Ltd, Bedwas House Industrial Estate, Bedwas, Newport, Gwent NP1 8XQ; Phone 01222 887333.

GOODFELLOW

These basses are made at the **Lowden** workshops in Northern Ireland. The distinctive long-top-horn/squat body shape is offered by the **Classic** (£995; five-string £1095; six-string £1295). It has 24-frets on an ebony board, two Armstrong humbuckers, triple-laminate body with pretty combinations of ash, maple, padauk, elm, walnut, mahogany and so on.
Contact: Goodfellow Guitars, 8 Glenford Way, Newtonards BT23 4BX, Northern Ireland; Phone: 01247 820542.

GRASS ROOTS

These Japanese newcomers have one bass available in the UK: the **SGB-550** (£449) with 21-frets, split & bar pickups, bolt-on-neck, maple body and chrome hardware.
Contact: Selectron UK Ltd, Springhead Enterprise Park, Gravesend, Kent DA11 8HD; Phone 01474 320445.

Goodfellow Classic

GRETSCH

The reintroduced far-eastern range from this vintage range includes a thin-hollow-body electro bass, called the **Broadcaster Bass** (£1485) and the similar **Electric-Acoustic Fretless** (£1099). The bound, single-cutaway body has spruce-top, maple back/sides body and a decorated 'triangular' soundhole, and the bridge has a built-in transducer feeding top-side volume and tone controls.
Contact: no UK distributor confirmed at time of going to press.

–The Bass Market–

GUILD

Two types of electro-acoustic basses are available. The **B4E** (£1055) has a single cutaway solid spruce top, oval soundhole, mahogany sides arched back, dot inlay on rosewood fingerboard, Guild Fishman professional, pre-amp and transducer; the **B4EHG** (£1095) has added high gloss finish. The **B30E** (£1599) features spruce top, mahogany back and sides, full size body and gold hardware; the **B30** (£1245) is the non-electronic version.

Contact: DJ Guitars, Division of Dixies Music, 2 Stocks Walk, Almondbury, Huddersfield HD5 8XB; Phone 01484 512601.

Hamer Impact five-string active

HAMER

This US-based manufacturer gives you more strings for your money. Their only four-string bass is the **Chaparral** (£1149), with a double cutaway, alder body, maple bolt-on-neck and split & bar pickups. The **Chaparral Five-string** (£1999) has a through-neck; as does the **Impact** (£1999), hand sculpted from exotic woods like African Sapelle, Purple Heart and Bolivian Rosewood, plus a unique 'film' transducer under the bridge and a separate active volume. The 30½in short scale **B12S Twelve-String** bass (£1649) and the 34in long scale option **B12L** (£1825) have twin EMG pickups, active bass and treble controls and all-maple construction.

Contact: Trace Elliot Ltd, Galliford Road, The Causeway, Maldon, Essex CM9 7XD; Phone 01621 851851.

HOHNER
Six bass types from this Korean brand are available here, the first four of which are 24-fretters. The **B2B** is a headless Steinberger copy having split & bar pickups feeding passive volume each and overall tone, and bolt-on-neck (£269). There's also a **B2A DB** (£379; left-handed £399) active version with stacked bass/treble control and active on/off switch, plus detunable bridge set-up. The **Jack Bass** is headless but with a 'real' body something like a Status. The **Jack Custom** (£419) has a Select bar humbucker feeding active on/off, two volumes, and stacked bass/treble. There's also a bolt-on-neck version (£229), fretless (£229) and a five-string (£449). The **B-Bass** (£399; five-string £429) has a similar body shape, pickups and controls but with two-tuners-a-side headstock and a DB detuner as standard. Last the 21-fretters: the **PJ Bass** (£219; left handed £229) has, you guessed, split & bar pickups and volume/volume/tone controls, and the **JJ Bass** (£319) has active twin Select humbuckers.
Contact: M Hohner Ltd, Bedwas House Industrial Estate, Bedwas, Newport, Gwent NP1 8XQ; Phone: 01222 887333.

IBANEZ
Korean ranges start with the 22-fret **TRB** series: **TRB50** (£249) has plywood body, single split pick-up, one-piece maple neck; **TRB100** (£319), alder body, split & bar pick-ups, black hardware (five-string **TRB105** £359); and **TRB200** (£369), ash body, split & bar pickups. The 24-fret, three-piece neck **SR** (or '**Soundgear**') series runs from the Korean-made, split & bar pickupped **SR400** (£349; fretless £359; five-string £399), and the active **SR500** (£479; left handed £489) to the more up-market Japanese SRs – the **SR800** (£699; five-string £775) has Resoncast body and three-band EQ. Top-of-the-range **SR1300** (£999; five-string £1129; six-string £1235) offers exotic hardwoods, five-piece neck and abalone inlays.
Contact: FCN, Morley Rd, Tonbridge, Kent TN9 1RA; Phone 01732 366421.

JACKSON
Five different Japanese-made 22-fret basses are available in this brand. The **Concert XL** (£639) has split & bar pickups and volume/balance/tone controls; **Concert V** five-string (£949) has active volume/bass/treble/balance controls. The **TBX** (£1649) has a curved through-neck body, comprising maple block and poplar wings and active

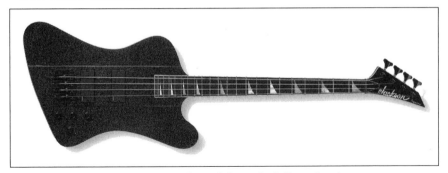

Jackson TBX: previous custom-only model now in full production

electronics and controls. The **Futura Ex** (£699) is specially designed for left-handers with split & bar humbucking pickups.
Contact: John Hornby Skewes & Co Ltd, Salem House, Parkinson Approach, Garforth, Leeds LS25 2HR; Phone 0113 2865381.

JIM HARLEY

Budget priced Korean-made brand has five basses on the market at present. The **PB20** (£165) has a split pickup and volume/tone controls, and the **JB50** (£180) has twin bar pickups, two volumes and a tone control. The other models are all 24-fret: the **TB30** (£200) has split & bar pickups, volume/tone/tone controls; the **SR40** (£250) one humbucking pickup; and the **HB40** (£325) is a Hofner Violin Bass copy with two humbucking pickups, two volumes and three switch controls.
Contact: Barnes & Mullins Ltd, 155 Grays Inn Road, London WC1X 8UF; Phone 0171 278 4631.

KEN SMITH

Having done much in the 1980s to popularise the five and six-string bass, this New York maker now offers a range of nine models, with hundreds of options involving exotic timbers, multi-piece bodies and advanced electronics. Basic models are: the top-of-the-line **BMT Elite 'G'** (£3245; add £50 for fives, £100 for sixes); **BT Custom 'G'** (£2895); **BT Custom 'M'** (£2445); **CR Custom 'G' Standard** (£1145); and **CR Custom 'M'** (£1795). The **Burner** series comprises the **Standard** (£1145), **Deluxe** (£1295), **Custom** (£1395), and **Artist** (£1645).
Contact: Bass Centre/House Music, 131 Wapping High Street, London E1 9NQ; Phone 0171 481 3350.

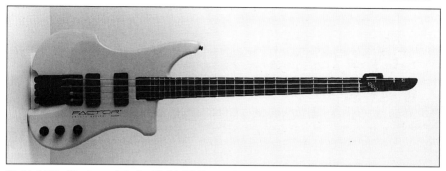

Kubicki Ex-Factor with the Kubicki Extension System to give two extra low frets

KUBICKI

Phillip Kubicki's basses come in three ranges: the **Factor** (£1895; fretless same price) has a laminated bolt-on maple neck, ebony fingerboard, soft maple body, twin humbuckers, switchable two-band active EQ, six-way preset tone control, plus unique Kubicki bridge-mounted tuning system. The **Ex-Factor** (£1895; fretless same) is basically identical, but for the Kubicki Extension System – a headstock-mounted, spring-loaded clasp securing the bottom string which can be flicked open to allow access to two more frets. The **Key Factor** (£1145; fretless same; five-string £1295) range has rosewood or maple board, conventional Schaller machineheads and adjustable bridge.
Contact: Bass Centre/House Music, 131 Wapping High Street, London E1 9NQ; Phone 0171 481 3350.

LARKIN

Irish-based company hand-building three bass models: all have 24 frets, two Chris Larkin/Kent Armstrong pickups, modular three-band active EQ. The **Reacter 'S'** (£1210+; fretlesses the same) is the four-string; the **5B** (£1300+) is the five; and the **Bassix** (£1400+) is, well guess.
Contact: Chris Larkin Custom, Castlegregory, Co Kerry, Ireland.

MARTIN

This American company is one of the oldest and most respected acoustic guitar makers in the business. They currently offer two four-string acoustic basses, the **B40** (£2500; all electronics +£300) and **B65** (£2400), with conventional round-soundhole and deep, waisted body. Both have an ebony fingerboard on mahogany neck (23 frets), and an ebony bridge on spruce top. The B65 has maple back and sides, white binding and black pickguard; the B40's back and sides are rosewood, and it has tortoiseshell-style binding and pickguard.

Contact: Dreadnought Guitar Co, No 68 New Caledonian Wharf, 6 Odessa Street, London SE16 1TN; Phone 0171 232 0778.

MODULUS GRAPHITE

MG founder Geoff Gould secured the original US patent for graphite guitar necks, and as you'd expect they're a consistent feature. His US-

Left: MusicMan StingRay 5; right: Overwater Progress six-string fretless

made **M92** (around £1299) has 24-frets with one powerful EMG humbucker and active circuitry; the **Quantum 4 SPi** basses (around £1499) have bodies with long sharp horns, 24-fret necks with phenolic fingerboard and twin EMG pickups, active circuitry and gold hardware. **Contact: The Bass & Drum Cellar, 23 Denmark Street, London WC2 H8NE; Phone 0171 240 3483.**

MUSICMAN

There are four US-made Ernie Ball MusicMan models available in the UK. The **StingRay** (£989) has a body of alder, ash or poplar, depending on finish, and 21-frets (with a pau ferro board for the fretless). A humbucker feeds volume, active and bass and treble (optional addition of active mid +£40). The five string **StingRay 5** (£1319) has a bigger scratchplate, ten-pole humbucker, 22-frets, and three-band EQ as standard plus series/single/parallel switch. The **Sterling** (£1069) strangely is a four-string version of the StingRay 5; and the six-string 'baritone guitar' **Silhouette** (£1569) has two DiMarzio split humbucking pickups and easy access 22-fret maple neck.
Contact: Strings & Things Ltd, Unit 2, 202-210 Brighton Road, Shoreham By Sea, W Sussex BN43 6RJ; Phone 0273 440442.

OVATION

Two US-made electro-acoustic options come from this well-known brand. The **Elite** (£1699; five-string £1769) has a solid spruce top, 24-fret ebony fingerboard, Lyracord deep bowl roundback body with cutaway and OP-X pre-amp; and the **Celebrity** (£649) is similar using less exotic wood.
Contact: TE Distribution, Galliford Road, The Causeway, Maldon, Essex CM9 7XD; Phone 01621 851851.

OVERWATER

British maker **Chris May** offers four distinctive through-neck design styles with Overwater pickups and active circuits: **Progress**, **Artisan**, **Fusion** and **Original**. Basic prices for any style, fretted or fretless, are in the ranges £795-£1350 (four-string), £895-£1575 (five) and £995-£1875 (six), and optional extras include bookmatched overlaid top (+£50), figured maple top (+£80), natural finish (+£50), gold hardware(+£45), and carbon graphite neck (+£250).
Contact: Overwater Guitar Co, Unit 7A, Haltwhistle Industrial Estate, Haltwhistle, Northumberland NE49 9JN; Phone 01434 321218.

PATRICK EGGLE

A complex (if surprisingly brief) history is behind this UK brandname. Suffice to say, after joining forces with Blade, eponymous young luthier Mr Eggle went off to launch a new guitar brand (Redwing), but, for some reason, his name lives on corporately (in the Fender tradition),

and is set to appear on at least one new bass model, produced in conjunction with designer Trevor Wilkinson, called the **New York Bass 4** (£599) - alder body, 22-fret bolt-on maple neck, Eggle humbucker, and 'full parametric active bass and treble tone network'.
Contact: The British Guitar Factory, Patrick Eggle Music Co Ltd, Bodmin Rd, Coventry CV2 5DB; Phone 01203 602895.

PEAVEY

It's hard to keep up with Peavey's enthusiastic output. In fact, as we write, their range is in the process of being updated again, so latest details and prices are patchy. There are eight distinct bass lines at present, all 21-fretters unless noted. The cheapest of the Peavey bass batch is the basic **Milestone** (£175), a 20-fretter with twin bar pickups; the **Foundation** (£249 maple board, £269 rosewood) has two single coils, two volumes and a tone control (five-string £349); while the **Forum** (*was* £329) has been upgraded, with a new Peavey VFL humbucker atop its light poplar body; the active **Forum Plus** (£429) has evolved into the **Forum AX**, which has two active humbuckers and heavy duty bridge, and there's a new **Forum V** too. The **Fury** (£285) has a split pickup feeding a volume and tone controls, while the **Axcelerator 5** (£569; fretless £519) has twin cutaway body, twin active humbucking pickups feeding volume, pan, stacked bass/treble boost and cut controls; the new upgraded **Axcelerator Plus** has light swamp ash body and pau ferro fingerboard, plus improved VFL humbuckers. The **TL-Five** (£999) and the **TL-Six** (£1429) 24-fret, five and six-stringers have graphite-reinforced through-necks, twin active pickups, active EQ with mid-range shift/cut boost, and mother-of-pearl inlays. The Brian Bromberg-designed **B-Quad 4** (£1650) has 24-frets, long sharp-horned body with a double-cutaway, graphite neck, phenolic fingerboard, active humbuckers with twin volume/tone controls plus master volume, four piezo bridge transducers with individual volume/tone control; there's also a new **B-Quad 5** five-string, with a 35in scale neck to give the low B better definition (available fretless, no extra charge). The **Cyberbass** (£1850), formerly the Midibase, is a bass-to-MIDI controller promising instant fret-contact-sensing pitch detection, plus twin active humbuckers, and 32 performance preset locations; the CyberBass Sound Module (£1099) offers lots more synth voices. There's also now a **Cyberbass 5**.
Contact: Peavey Electronics (UK) Ltd, Hatton House, Hunters Road, Corby, Northants NN17 5JE; Phone 01536 205520.

Rickenbacker 4004 Laredo: low loss circuitry

PEDULLA

Made in Massachussetts, the Pedulla bass has distinctive super-thin sculpted body horns. The **MVP/Buzz** series comes as **Deluxe, Custom A, Custom AA, Signature AAA** and **Limited Edition** versions (**MVP/Buzz** four-strings £1495–£2195; **MVP5/PentaBuzz** five-strings £1695–£2445; **MVP6/HexaBuzz** six-strings £1845–£2795; **MVP8/ OctaBuzz** eight-strings £1695–£2445). The **T-Series Thunderbass/ Thunderbuzz** basses come as **Custom** and **Signature** options: **T4** four strings (£1795 & £1995); **T5** five-strings (£1995 & £2195); **T6** six-strings (£2145 & £2345); **T8** eight-strings (£1995 & £2195); there's also a more exotic **ET** series (£1995–£2195). The **Mark Egan Signature** series has a standard shape, twin bar pickups and deep cutaways: **ME4** (£1995); **ME5** (£2195); **ME4F+8** double-neck (£4345). And lots of options. **Contact: The Bass Centre/House Music, 131 Wapping High Street, London E1 9NQ; Phone 0171 265 1567.**

RICKENBACKER

This veteran guitar-maker from California has been producing distinctive electric basses for over 30 years. There are currently two standards types – both solids – and two limited editions in the UK (add £117 for left-handers). First of the standards is the **4003** – the traditional Ricky 'hook-horn' shape body with 20 frets, stereo circuit, bound body/neck and triangle fingerboard markers (£1159); the range

–The Bass Market–

includes **4003S** mono, unbound, dot markers, (£1069), and **4003S/5** five-string (£1249) or **4003S/8** eight-string (£1455) and **4003 Fretless** (£1159). The **4004 Cheyenne** and **4004 Laredo** (both £1275) have low loss circuit design and twin bar humbucking pickups. Second standard type is a modern double-away, two-pickup solid with 20 frets, and 'semi-active' controls, available either as the **2030 Hamburg** (£895) or the bound, gold-hardware-equipped **2050 El Dorado** (£1069). The limited editions are both traditional Ricky designs, the **4001CS Chris Squire** model with Squire's favoured neck profile, cream lacquer finish, and signed scratchplate (£1365), and **2030 Glenn Frey** (£935) with maple body, neck, fingerboard and twin humbucking pickups.
Contact: Rosetti Ltd, 4 Tamdown Way, Springwood Industrial Estate, Braintree, Essex CM7 7QL; Phone 01376 550033.

ROCKWOOD

One Chinese-made model, the **LX90** (£129), with basswood body, maple neck, split pickup, predictable shape.
Contact: M Hohner Ltd, Bedwas House Industrial Estate, Bedwas, Newport, Gwent NP1 8XQ; Phone: 01222 887333.

Left: Sei bass from Martin Petersen; right: rear view of body and thru-neck detail

SADOWSKY
New York builder offering: **Standard** (alder body £1995; swamp ash £2195; five-string, EMG pickups, £2595) with bolt-on 21-fret maple neck and two active pickups (figured maple top £300 extra).
Contact: The Bass Centre/House Music, 131 Wapping High Street, London E1 9NQ; Phone 0171 265 1567.

SEI
British-based custom maker **Martin Petersen**'s attractive basses have a wenge/maple headless (headed +£50) through-neck, a sharp-horned body of exotic wood facing maple, and twin Bartolini or Kent Armstrong pickups feeding volume, pan and active treble, mid and bass controls. Sei basses come in four, five and six-string variants, ranging from about £1200 to some £1900.
Contact: Sei Bass, The Gallery, 142 Royal College Street, Camden, London NW1 0TA; Phone 0171 267 5458.

SIGMA
Korean-made bargain priced copies of Martin acoustic basses, with the **STB-M** and the **STB-R** (both £299) offering rosewood back and sides or maple back and sides respectively, plus on-board electronics.
Contact: Dreadnought Guitar Co, No 68 New Caledonian Wharf, 6 Odessa Street, London SE16 1TN; Phone 0171 232 0778.

STATUS
There are six series now available from this British maker, mostly solid body instruments with Status pickups and graphite necks. All have active circuits, of varied layout and facility, apart from the single-pickup 'entry level' **Shark** (£549; five-string £699). The **Energy** (£699; add £150 to prices for five-string, £300 for six-strings) are bolt-on-neck, and the **Energy Artist** (£899) offers a bookmatched maple or walnut laminated body. The smaller, 20-fret, contoured double cutaway **Eclipse** (£999) has natural wood or gloss finishes, and **Eclipse Artist** (£1149) has twin pickup/two-band active configuration. The rest are through-necks, with bolt-on options: the **Stealth** (£1699) is the only one with an all-graphite body; the **Empathy** (£1799) has an 11-piece exotic wood body with custom finish options, and is now the only Status model that's available headless. The **Electro** semi-solid (£1199) features mahogany back with slash-holed maple top, double cutaway, piezo pickups and active controls, not to mention nylon flatwound strings.

Steinberger Q4: four/five-string, fretted/fretless, active/passive, DB detuner options

Contact: TE Distribution, Galliford Road, Maldon, The Causeway, Essex CM9 7XD; Phone 01621 851851.

STEINBERGER

This US maker popularised headless and almost bodyless basses; now they offer two types of bass in the UK. The **XL** (from £1425) features a conventional (for Steinberger) body shape; and the **Q** model (from £1155), is a 'Kubicki-like' design. There are various options – four/five string, fretless/fretted, passive/active, and Steinberger's DB string detuner on the **Pro** variants – which alter the basic prices shown.
Contact: Omec Distribution, 21 Denmark Street, London WC2H 8HW; Phone 0171 240 8292.

STUART SPECTOR DESIGN

The man considered with Ned Steinberger to be 'the father of modern bass design' has three separate manufacturing sources, all devoted to through-neck instruments. The Korean **NS-94** (£599; five-string £699) has through-neck, soft maple body, split & bar pickups and active electronics, while the European (Czech) **NS-4CR** (from £1295; five-string +£100) adds a two-piece maple body, mother of pearl inlay on rosewood fingerboard, and gold hardware. The US **SD** series (from £2495) is similar but handbuilt by Spector himself, offering many options including piezo bridge, fibre optics and finish variations.

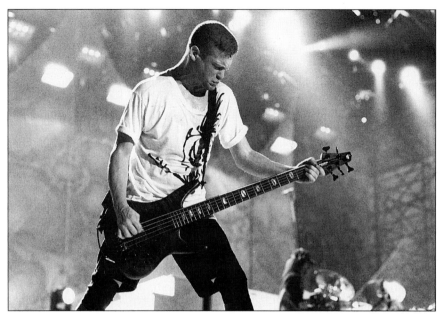

Spector five-string being put through its paces by Metallica's Jason Newsted

Contact: DGC Distribution Ltd, Unit 20, Enterprise City, Green Lane, Spennymoor, Durham, County Durham DH1 4ED; Phone 01388 810300.

TAKAMINE

One bass model for this renowned Japanese acoustic maker: the **Jasmine ES100 CM** (£435) is an electro-acoustic with maple top, back and sides, with cutaway and bound fingerboard (£435).

Contact: Korg UK Ltd, 8-9 The Crystal Centre, Elmgrove Road, Harrow, Middlesex HA1 2YR; Phone 0181 427 5377.

TANGLEWOOD

Several different model styles from this Korean brand are sold here: a straightforward 21-fret split pickup model, the **FPB 24 Outlaw** (£159); the long-scale **TSB 403 Lonewolf** (£199; left-hander +£20; fretless +£25), and the jazzy **Nevada II Super** (£199; left-hander same price). Imitations continue with the **RVB2 Violin Bass** (£349; essential left-hander +£30); the **Eclipse**, with slim bull horn laminated body with a double cutaway and split & bar pickups (£229; five-string £249); the

–The Bass Market–

Peacemaker II (£449; left-hander £485) has split & bar pickups feeding active EQ; while the **Baron** (£499; left-hander £539) has through-neck design and more elaborate woodwork. The electro-acoustic **Allouette** (£399) has a spruce top, maple neck, back/sides and a Fishman pickup with four-band EQ.
Contact: European Music Company Ltd, Main Road, Biggin Hill, Kent TN16 3YN; Phone 01959 571600.

TOBIAS

Six ranges are available here from this US maker. The **Pro** (£705; five-string £765; six-string £825) offers 24-fret maple through-neck construction. The **Deluxe** (£529, five-string £559; six-string £589) has twin bar pickups, active treble/bass boost/cut and volume and pan controls. The **Killer B** (£1785; coloured option +£145; five-string £1859; six-string £1929) has bolt-on maple neck (**Special** version has wenge neck at £1429), twin 'bar' pickups and three-band EQ. The **Basic** (£2215; five-string £2355; six-string £2499) has options of various attractive woods for the hand-carved body wings, plus twin Bartolini pickups and Bartolini active circuit (two volumes, three tones). The **Classic** is the same design but with more elaborate woodworking (£1425; five-string £2569; six-string £2715). And finally the **Signature** (£3495; five-string £3709; six-string £3855) uses even more exotic woods.
Contact: Omec Distribution, 21 Denmark Street, London WC2H 8NE; Phone 0171 240 8292.

TUNE

Three ranges from this Japanese brand are sold here. The **Bass Maniac** (£1079; five-string £1225) has maple body, split & bar pickups feeding volume, pan and two tones, bolt-on neck boasting no fewer than 25 frets. The **STB** bass (£739; five-string £879; transparent colours +£50) is similar; while the **'King Bass' TWB Wood** series have curvy bodies with lovely figured maple on mahogany, twin bars feeding volume/pan and three-way EQ, and fretted or semi-acoustic fretless bolt-on necks (£1445; five-string £1575; six-string £1699).
Contact: no UK distributor confirmed at time of going to press.

VANTAGE

There are two models from this Korean brand: the **YB 350** (£175), with one split pickup and rosewood fingerboard; and the electro-acoustic **VB**

Tune King Bass TWB Wood series five and six-string models

25SCE (£485) with ovankol back/sides, solid cedar top and a peizo pickup.
Contact: Korg UK, 8-9 The Crystal Centre, Elmgrove Road, Harrow, Middx HA1 2YR; Phone 0181 427 5377.

<u>VESTER</u>
Another Korean manufacturer building quality budget basses. The **VB2205** (£199) is a Fenix-like jazzish bass, in the expected style; while the **Clipper** series comprises the **VB11** (£299) with maple body and two -octave, five-piece maple neck, active twin bar pickups, two volumes and tone control; the **VB13** (£299) is the fretless version. The **VB1435EQ** (£389) is described as an 'Aria-like' solid body rock bass with split and bar pickups.
Contact: Sound Control, 73 Elgin Street, Fife KY12 6SD; Phone 01383 733353.

–The Bass Market–

WAL

There are four clearly defined models in this British maker's twin-pickup range: the **Standard** bass (£1345+) is a 21-fret four-string with

A shot from the Warwick family album

Wal's fine active set-up (volume, pan, bass and treble, pull-pots for presence and harmonic boost). The **Two-Octave** bass (£1456+) has 24 frets and a longer-horn body shape, also shared by the **Five-String** (£1640) and the recently added **Six-String** (£2138+). Many options.
Contact: Electric Wood, Sandown Works, Chairborough Road, High Wycombe, Bucks HP12 3HH; Phone 01494 442925.

WARWICK

Seven main styles are available in the UK from this prolific German maker: **Fortress, Corvette, Streamer, Thumb, Dolphin, Buzzard** and the electro-acoustic **Alien**. The first two have bolt-on necks only, while the last three are solely through-neck construction; all have wenge fingerboards. The **Fortress One** (£845; fretless same price) has split & bar pickups; the five-string version (£950) has twin bar pickups. The **Corvette Proline** (£925) has twin J pickups feeding one volume/active control, pan, and stacked bass/treble; the five-string version (£1132) has split & bar pickups and the six-stringer (£1390) has active electronics. The bolt-on version of the **Streamer** (£1161; five-string £1289; six-string £1537), has active split & bar pickups (twin humbuckers on the six) feeding volume/active, pan, treble and bass. The through-neck **Streamer Stage I** has active split & bar pickups (twin bars on the six) feeding stacked volume/active, pan, mid, treble and bass (£1459; five-string £2232; six-string £2533); the **Stage II** versions have twin bar pickups and classier woodwork (£1919; five-string £2178). The bolt-on neck version of the **Thumb** (£1799; five-string £2061; six-string £2469), has split & bar pickups (twin humbuckers on the six); while the **Through-neck Thumb** is a 26-fretter (for those tricky super-high As), with two active bar pickups on the four (£1799), five (£2061) and six-string (£2469, with twin humbuckers) versions. The **Dolphin** is another 26-fretter with an angled pickup at the neck and humbucker at the bridge (£2082; five-string £2508). The **Alien** (£2283) is a strange-looking electro-acoustic bass (spruce top; ovankol back/sides) with an asymmetric soundhole positioned above the end of the neck, and a flamboyantly-shaped bridge with built-in piezo pickup; the top-mounted control panel includes a trim volume for each string, as well as gain, treble, mid and bass.
Contact: Music & Audio Distribution Ltd, 10 Station Parade, Willesden Green, London NW2 4NH; Phone 0181 452 1009.

WASHBURN

This US-owned far eastern-built brand offers the solid, 24-fret, bolt-on-neck **XB** series, and an **electro** range. The passive **XB200** (£299) has split & bar pickups and simple volume and tone controls; the active **XB400** (£399) has an alder body, twin humbucking pickups, two volumes, tone and selector; the **XB500** (£439) and the **XB600** (£499) are the five and six-string versions with twin J pickups; and the **XB800** (£499) has Status hardware, pickups and circuitry. Washburn did much to establish the idea of the electro-acoustic bass with the 24-fret **AB** series, with distinctive diagonal-slot soundhole. The Korean **AB30** (£699) has 23-frets, book matched sycamore top, sides and

Yamaha RBX350II: the RBX is one of four bass ranges currently available

back, Equis II preamp system and Fishman pickup, ebony board and gold hardware; the similar but less well-appointed electro models are the **AB20** (£599) and **AB10** (£499).
Contact: Washburn UK Ltd, Amor Way, Letchworth, Herts SG6 1UG; Phone 01462 482466.

YAMAHA
There are currently four bass ranges available from this far-eastern brand: **RBX**, **BB**, **Attitude** and **TRB** (all 22-fret unless noted). The basic **RBX250II** (£239; fretless same price) has a split pickup feeding

volume and tone; the **RBX350II** (£299; left-hander same price) has scalloped cutaways, split & bar pickups, volume, tone and pan; while the **RBX1000** (£749) has 24 frets, contoured, streamlined ash body, with split & bar pickups feeding volume, bass, treble and pan controls. The **BB350** (£369; fretless same price; left-hander +£40) has 21 frets, twin bar pickups feeding two volumes and tone controls; the **BB1500A** (£639) has 21-frets, active three-band EQ controls, and gold hardware. The **BB5NE 'Nathan East' Model** (£1699), has 24-fret ebony fingerboard, figured maple/alder body and twin double-coil pickups. The **Attitude Standard** (£499; five-string £599) has 21-frets, split & bar pickups, volume, tone and selector; and the **Special** version (£399) has 21 frets, DiMarzio 'woofer' and split pickups. The **TRB** basses are Yamaha's prime range, featuring 24-fret through-necks, scalloped cutaways, twin single-coils, versatile five-control active circuits, and gold hardware, in four (£939), five (£999; fretless same price) and six-string (£1049). The **TRB-P** basses also have two single coil piezo pickups and maple/ mahogany necks, in four (£1299), five (£1469) and six-string (£1569); while the **TRB-JP 'John Patitucci' Model** (£1699) is a six-string with twin double cois and figured maple/ash/alder body.
Contact: Yamaha-Kemble Music (UK) Ltd, Sherbourne Drive, Tilbrook, Milton Keynes MK7 8BL; Phone 01908 366700.

ZON

This Californian maker specialises in graphite-necked basses: cheapest is the **Sonus** (£1375; five-string £1595; six-string £1795) – 24 frets, bolt-on neck, two-piece ash body, single coil pickups and active EQ; the **Sonus Special** (add £220 to above prices) has bubinga top and multi-coil pickups with enhanced low-mid response. The **Legacy Standard** (£1595; five-string £1845; six-string £1995) is similar but with dual coil pickups and ZP-2 electronics. the **Legacy Elite** (£1995–£2795) has a fixed graphite neck, with bookmatched top or custom colours. The extraordinary **Michael Manring Hyperbass** has a three-octave fretless fingerboard, single humbucker and ZP-2S EQ. **Version I** (£2395) has non-detunable keys or bridge; **Version II** £3695) has detunable keys and bridge; while **Version III** (£5895) also has a quad/mono piezo pickup.
Contact: The Bass Centre/House Music, 131 Wapping High Street, London E1 9NQ; Phone 0171 265 1567.

WHAT NOW?

So where to go from here? Laurence Canty stops playing for a while, takes in some bass books, watches a few choice videos, and analyses the pros and cons of lessons and classes

Really, the only way to learn to play bass is by playing it. But of course it helps to be a little prepared before going in at the deep end. So what help is there to hand?

BOOKS

There are two things that can be stated with reasonable certainty on the subject of bass books:
1) There's a lot of them.
2) Most of them don't deserve shelf space.

So to save you much time, energy, and money, here's a list of books we feel are worth considering.

LAURENCE CANTY: ELECTRIC BASS GUITAR – £10.95
I'd like to say that this is a pearl of 20th century literature, but I'm really too modest. *(Actually it is an excellent bass tutor, honest – Ed)*

JOHN DEWITT: RHYTHMIC FIGURES FOR BASSISTS
Currently difficult to find, this two-volume set provides plenty of

–What Now?–

examples to practise your reading skills, so check the library.

DAN DEAN: ELECTRIC BASS; THE STUDIO BASSIST
Each title comes in three volumes (£4.95 apiece) and provides a wide range of varied material, although some of the examples are a little odd.

GUITAR PLAYER: BASS HEROES – £14.95
Thirty bassists – including James Jamerson and Jaco Pastorius – reveal all in this comprehensive compilation of interviews.

JOE HUBBARD: BASSLINES; POP BASSLINES – £5.95 each
Again, accurate titles. The first volume is a collection of lines by Mark King, Stanley Clarke, Marcus Miller, and Jaco Pastorius. The second includes Pino Palladino, Nathan East, Bernard Edwards, Louis Johnson, and Sting. Not for the beginner, requiring both technical and reading skills.

CAROL KAYE: ELECTRIC BASS LINES COMPLETE
The first volume of this six-part series was originally published 20 years ago and was later repackaged in two parts. Again, reading skills necessary.

MAKING MUSIC: WHAT BASS – you know this one, don't you?
Everything you wanted to know but were afraid to ask; even includes the all-inclusive book list.

ADAM NOVRICK: HARMONICS FOR ELECTRIC BASS – £9.95
Useful reference, although it does go on a bit.

JACO PASTORIUS: MODERN ELECTRIC BASS – £6.95 or £18.95 w/cassette
Best read in conjunction with the video (see below).

RUFUS REID: THE EVOLVING BASSIST – £19.95
MIKE RICHMOND: MODERN WALKING BASS TECHNIQUE
CHUCK SHER: THE IMPROVISER'S BASS METHOD
These three books, whose authors' names come conveniently together near the end of the alphabet, are recommended if you want to play jazz.

ALLAN SLUTSKY (DOCTOR LICKS):
STANDING IN THE SHADOWS OF MOTOWN (THE LIFE AND MUSIC OF LEGENDARY BASSIST JAMES JAMERSON) – £24.95
Absolutely essential for the transcriptions alone. The accompanying cassettes (or CDs) have Jamerson's lines re-recorded by a star line-up, indicating his importance in bass history – they include Jack Bruce, John Entwistle, Anthony Jackson, Will Lee, Marcus Miller, Pino Palladino, John Patitucci, and Chuck Rainey. Expensive, but lots to learn.

122

I could also add...

BARRY GREEN: THE INNER GAME OF MUSIC

Something a little different, and not specifically a bass book. However, it could just change your life and enable you to get closer to your musical potential.

Videos generally tend to promise more than they deliver

VIDEOS

Videos are far more expensive than a typical book and in general they are disappointing. Only one is essential viewing:

JACO PASTORIUS: MODERN ELECTRIC BASS (85 MINUTES) – £30.95

A flawed masterpiece, but an invaluable insight into Jaco's musical and technical approach. Something for everyone, not just Pastorius fans/clones. Bassist Jerry Jemmott asks the right questions and gives the conversation direction and structure without becoming formal or humourless. What we need now to complement this is the video of Joni Mitchell's live set 'Shadows And Light' – it exists, it's been shown on BBC, and is available on video in the US (on Warner Bros).

Others worth considering are:

EARL GRECO: STAR LICKS – £13.85

There's slap, snap and tap, harmonics and two-handed chords.

JOHN PATITUCCI: ELECTRIC BASS Pt1 & Pt2 – £30.95 EACH

PAUL WESTWOOD: THE COMPLETE BASS GUITAR PLAYER – £12.99

–WHAT NOW?–

MAGAZINES

The annual cost will be less than a couple of private lessons or a bass video, and you'll doubtless get more information.

BASS PLAYER (US)
£2.75 – eight issues/year
BASSICS (CANADA)
£3.25 – three issues/year
BASSIST (UK)
£1.95 – 12 issues/year
MAKING MUSIC (UK)
£15 for 12-month subscription. The best musicians' magazine, even if we say it ourselves, with a monthly *Bass Case* especially for deep musicians (Tel: 0171 405 2055)

LESSONS

I was self-taught (which actually means learning by doing), and now I combine teaching and playing. So I can see the pros and cons of having lessons. Finding out for yourself is rewarding and can mean a better understanding, but it takes longer. You may waste a lot of time by doing something wrong, and then have to relearn it, which wastes even more time. You may feel that tuition will cramp your style and interfere with your self-expression, but that depends on your attitude and the teacher's approach.

What is becoming increasingly evident is that the top players tend to have a musical background, perhaps by having played another instrument from an early age. So these bassists not only have technical skills, but musical knowledge and reading ability as well. Lessons should help you to achieve similar standards – but don't see them as a substitute for playing experience. What you learn needs to be put into practice, or it becomes academic.

Finding a teacher involves checking ads in the music press and in local music shops. Obviously someone nearby is convenient so a call to the local branch of the Musicians' Union could produce results – for example there are over 50 bass teachers listed just in the Union's current *London District Directory*. The other practical consideration is 'How much?' Well, the MU rate for teaching is £17 an hour (revised

Organisations like BIT (see over) hold clinics where you can learn from skilled players at close quarters; this one featured Graham Edwards (right) of Go West

every September), so anyone charging less is a cad and a bounder, and anyone charging more is either a scoundrel or has something special to offer.

Having got some numbers to call, how do you figure out whether it's worth booking a lesson? Apart from the obvious questions, people tend to ask, 'Who've you played with?' Not relevant, really. Touring the world with a name band is not a teaching qualification, and excesses on the road may have left the teacher incapable of stringing words together into sentences. More sensible questions would be, 'Who've you taught?' or, 'What teaching experience have you got?' One final suggestion would be to avoid the guitar teacher who also teaches bass – would you go to a violin teacher if you wanted to learn cello? So if a lesson seems worthwhile, book an hour and see how it goes. You'll know whether or not it's worth continuing.

An alternative to private lessons, though only in London as far as we know, is to go to a bass class. Here's the basic information on each – we suggest you get in touch if interested and get more detail on what they have to offer. You'll have to make up your own mind as to whether or not this approach is for you.

Another BIT clinic, this time featuring John Patitucci and Frank Gambale

BASS INSTITUTE OF TECHNOLOGY (0171 265 0284)

Opened in 1987, and known for a while as the Bass Academy, BIT is situated above the Bass Centre shop in east London. Courses cater for beginners to advanced players, and there are several options to choose from: two-hours/week for ten weeks (£165); six hours/week for ten weeks (£340); one-year full time course (40 weeks, approx £3500); or private tuition at £20/hour.

BASSTECH (0181 740 1031)

Opened in 1989, they also offer lessons for all levels and styles: two hours/week for ten weeks (£169); ten week full-time certificate course (£995); two year HE diploma course (£6800, but grant-funded); or private teaching at £16/hour. Workshops offer interchange between BassTech, DrumTech and Guitar Institute students; audio visual lab produces accompanying teaching vids.

GOLDSMITHS COLLEGE (0171 919 7200)

Bass course started in 1975 and consists of three-hour classes held on Saturdays from September each year. Levels 1&2 are 12-week courses (£44 each); levels 3&4 are 30 weeks (£162 each).

For more on educational establishments, and learning in general, see the Learning Special in *Making Music* issue 99 (June 1994).

AT LAST...

So, you've bought the bass, the amp and the books, watched the video, and had the lessons. What should you do next?

Rather than just devoting yourself to your band, why not get involved in other projects? Playing with different musicians demands a different approach and will help you play better. If your only outlet is a rock band, then you probably won't develop such skills as improvising or reading music, which can help make you a better musician and so a better bassist.

Your most important skill is creating basslines which fit the song so well, you can't imagine it without them. Developing that skill is largely a matter of experience. Don't just copy other players – absorb influences so they become a part of your personal style.

And let us know how you get on, OK?